2ND Edition

BEST TENT
Camping

ARIZONA

YOUR CAR-CAMPING GUIDE TO SCENIC BEAUTY, THE SOUNDS
OF NATURE, AND AN ESCAPE FROM CIVILIZATION

To Duane and Sarah Phillips

Best Tent Camping: Arizona

Published by Menasha Ridge Press
Printed in the United States of America
Distributed by Publishers Group West
Second edition, first printing

Library of Congress Cataloging-in-Publication Data for this book is available at catalog.loc.gov.
ISBN: 978-1-63404-076-1; eISBN: 978-1-63404-077-8

Project editor: Ritchey Halphen
Cover and interior design: Jonathan Norberg
Maps: Steve Jones and Kirstin Olmon Phillips
Photos: Kirstin Olmon Phillips and Kelly Phillips, except where noted
Copy editor: Kerry Smith
Proofreader: Vanessa Lynn Rusch
Indexer: Meghan Miller Brawley/Potomac Indexing

MENASHA RIDGE PRESS
An imprint of AdventureKEEN
2204 First Ave. S., Ste. 102
Birmingham, AL 35233

Visit menasharidge.com for a complete listing of our books and for ordering information. Contact us at our website, at facebook.com/menasharidge, or at twitter.com/menasharidge with questions or comments. To find out more about who we are and what we're doing, visit blog.menasharidge.com.

Front cover: The View Campground (campground 9, page 39); *cover inset and opposite:* The Flatiron from Lost Dutchman State Park Campground (campground 19, page 70)

2ND Edition

BEST △ TENT
Camping

ARIZONA

YOUR CAR-CAMPING GUIDE TO SCENIC BEAUTY, THE SOUNDS
OF NATURE, AND AN ESCAPE FROM CIVILIZATION

Kirstin Olmon Phillips
Kelly Phillips

MENASHA RIDGE PRESS
Your Guide to the Outdoors Since 1982

Arizona Campground Locator Map

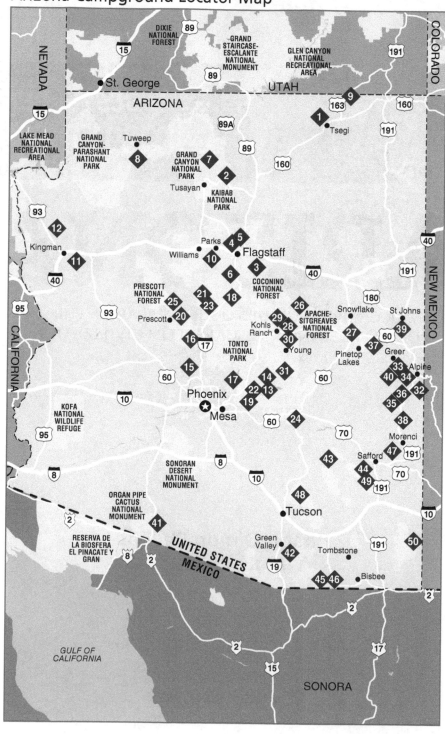

CONTENTS

MOGOLLON RIM 91

WHITE MOUNTAINS 110

SOUTHERN ARIZONA 138

Map Legend

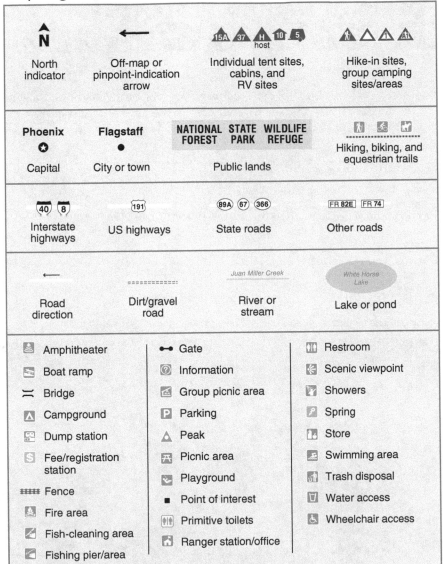

North indicator

Off-map or pinpoint-indication arrow

Individual tent sites, cabins, and RV sites

Hike-in sites, group camping sites/areas

Phoenix — Capital

Flagstaff — City or town

NATIONAL FOREST STATE PARK WILDLIFE REFUGE — Public lands

Hiking, biking, and equestrian trails

Interstate highways

US highways

State roads

Other roads

Road direction

Dirt/gravel road

River or stream — *Juan Miller Creek*

Lake or pond — *White Horse Lake*

- Amphitheater
- Boat ramp
- Bridge
- Campground
- Dump station
- Fee/registration station
- Fence
- Fire area
- Fish-cleaning area
- Fishing pier/area

- Gate
- Information
- Group picnic area
- Parking
- Peak
- Picnic area
- Playground
- Point of interest
- Primitive toilets
- Ranger station/office

- Restroom
- Scenic viewpoint
- Showers
- Spring
- Store
- Swimming area
- Trash disposal
- Water access
- Wheelchair access

ACKNOWLEDGMENTS

We would like to acknowledge all of the U.S. Forest Service and park rangers and volunteers who make our public lands work, and who must be doing it for love (it can't be the money). Thanks for sharing your stories with us.　　—Kirstin Olmon Phillips and Kelly Phillips

A uniquely Arizonan tent site at Yavapai Campground (campground 25, page 88)

PREFACE

As our plane made its bumpy arrival at Sky Harbor International Airport, the kid next to us frowned while looking out across the runway and mumbled resentfully, "I hate Arizona. It's so brown."

We exchanged wry smiles, hearing the echo of so many other voices, even some long-term Phoenicians we know. Later we mulled over the injustice of it. Obviously, this boy has never camped by the rushing Black River or seen the broad meadows and towering pines above the North Rim of the Grand Canyon. We planned exactly where we'd take this poor, misguided youth to show him just how green this state can be: up to the verdant crowns of the southern sky islands, the Chiricahuas, Pinaleños, Santa Ritas, Santa Catalinas, Huachucas; along the emerald riparian corridors of the Verde, Gila, and San Pedro Rivers; and into the cool forests of the Mogollon Rim and the White Mountains.

Then we'd bring that kid to the desert again, to reveal to him the kaleidoscope of hues that look brown from an airplane window. In the spring, we'd hike him around the Superstitions and to Lake Pleasant to show him hillsides carpeted in yellow as the Mexican gold poppies and brittlebush bloom, and dotted with purple lupines and orange and pink globemallows. He'd see the startling fuchsia, crimson, and lemon yellow of cholla, hedgehog, and prickly pear flowers against deep-green cactus skins. Finally, we'd make a grand tour of Sedona, Sycamore Canyon, the Painted Desert, and the Grand Canyon, to see all the vivid colors of the earth itself.

We have no idea who that boy was or how he ended up spending his time in Arizona, but this book is for him and all the kids out there like him.

Perhaps you're a visitor from elsewhere, or maybe you're a new Arizona resident wondering what you've gotten yourself into. If metro Phoenix is your main frame of reference, you might be forgiven for having some misgivings. There's an old joke that Arizona has only two seasons, hot and hotter, but cheer up—you can find spring, summer, winter, or fall within a 5-hour drive at almost any time of the year. Somewhere in Arizona, there's a landscape and a climate to please almost everybody.

What we've tried to do in this guide is help you find those places that will suit you best. We're making a few assumptions along the way: that you love the outdoors, that you favor peace and quiet but are sometimes willing to compromise, and that you appreciate a wide variety of different experiences. In short, that you're a lot like us.

Like so many Arizonans, we're imports from other climes—Kirstin from the lakes and snows of Minnesota and Kelly from the lush hills of Maryland. Kirstin knew from day one that she belonged here, while Kelly took some time to develop a full appreciation of the desert. Family camping played a part of both our young lives, in tents, pop-ups, and cabins. The leap to camping as adults came for both of us when we moved to the Grand Canyon State, where unparalleled natural diversity calls out to be explored.

Studies have shown that being in nature is good for your body and soul. This just makes sense in our modern world of superhighways and smartphones. Congratulations on making the effort to tear yourselves (and especially your kids) away from comfy chairs and glowing screens!

Note also that these preserves and parks and wildlands need you as much as you need them. This is still an era of budget squeezing and struggling to make ends meet for the U.S. Forest Service, the National Park Service, and state and county parks, even as the number of people seeking recreation in America's outdoors increases every year. Those of us who cherish these resources need to support them, to raise awareness of their value, to advocate their wise use, and to raise another generation of responsible, educated, and enthusiastic campers—kids who get excited when they look out the airplane window.

WHAT'S NEW

We wrote the first edition of this book just before the 2008 economic crash, which had a significant impact on many of Arizona's recreational sites. It's been interesting to see how various agencies have responded: some sites have closed, some sites have removed their campground hosts, and some sites have increased their prices, although a surprising number of sites have remained free.

We've added several new campgrounds for the second edition, including one at Monument Valley that puts the iconic view of the Mittens just outside your tent. At Ashurst Lake, you'll find great fishing and bird-watching opportunities with a view of the San Francisco Peaks in the distance. Brookchar offers walk-in tent-only sites with sunset views across Big Lake. Creekside Lawrence Crossing, named for a murdered man, is now a green and peaceful base to experience the far more ancient past at the V Bar V petroglyph site.

We've also added remote gems like verdant and often-unused Rose Creek in the gorgeous Sierra Anchas, as well as popular Sunny Flat, a perfect setting for bird-watching and exploring the unique geology of the Chiricahua Mountains. For desert bikers and hikers, we've included the sprawling, spectacular McDowell Mountain County Park outside of Phoenix.

Prices, websites, and profile text have all been updated to reflect the changes that have occurred over the past 10 years. New categories for the best campgrounds include the best sites for each season, the best free sites, and the best sites to see wildflowers and birds.

What *hasn't* changed is the rich history that you get to experience by visiting these campgrounds and the never-ending beauty that is the state of Arizona.

—Kirstin and Kelly

BEST CAMPGROUNDS

BEST FOR CANOEING AND KAYAKING

BEST FOR SWIMMING

BEST FOR SUMMER

BEST FOR WINTER

BEST FOR BIRD-WATCHING

BEST FOR FAMILIES

BEST FOR SCENIC VISTAS AND PHOTOGRAPHY

BEST FREE CAMPGROUNDS

BEST FOR WILDFLOWERS

BEST HIDDEN GEMS

Saguaros keep watch from the hills above Canyon Lake as you paddle out to The Point (see campground 22, page 79).

INTRODUCTION

HOW TO USE THIS GUIDEBOOK

Menasha Ridge Press welcomes you to *Best Tent Camping: Arizona.* Whether you're new to camping or you've been sleeping in your portable shelter over decades of outdoor adventures, please review the following information. It explains how we have worked with the author to organize this book and how you can make the best use of it.

CHOOSING THE TOP 50

Because we've written this book with car campers in mind, we've chosen to include only campgrounds that you can drive to, with the exception of one boat-access-only campground. Another book entirely could be written about the best backpacking camps in Arizona, but we haven't included any of those here. Rather, we've included only official public campgrounds, striving for an equal balance of the developed and undeveloped. One of us must have her shower every day and the other would be perfectly happy to hang out in the woods for weeks, so we think we represent both ends of the spectrum.

When we told other campers we were writing this book, smiles would cross their faces as they thought about their personal favorite places to pitch a tent. More often than not, if they chose to share their secret with us (knowing that we might reveal it to the public), they knew of a great location on public land with no more amenities than a fire ring and a great view.

A startlingly high proportion of Arizona is public land, belonging to the U.S. Forest Service (USFS), the Bureau of Land Management, or the State of Arizona, and most of this is open to dispersed camping: choose your own spot off the road or trail, maybe where someone else has camped or maybe not, with no fee, no facilities, no trash—strictly pack in/pack out. The wilderness is at your doorstep, and you may be all alone.

Again, we leave it to you to discover Arizona's backcountry on your own. USFS rangers tell us that many campers just want to know where they can camp for free and don't care about amenities or ambience. While such campers aren't our target audience, we have included a number of free campgrounds and a few dispersed camping areas.

We narrowed our choices among Arizona's many great campgrounds based on a number of factors. We divided the state into regions and looked for campgrounds that made an effort to give tent campers something special, whether it be walk-in sites that have great lake views, tent-only sections separated from the RVs, or other possibilities such as tenting on the beach. In some regions we found *too many* great options, but we did our best to distill them to the ones we felt would be best for tenters.

We looked for smaller campgrounds—the smaller the campground, the less likely a 30-foot fifth wheel will be your neighbor. Of course, the pioneer spirit is still alive and well in the West, and that means there's no road so long or so rough that someone won't drag a trailer down it. You may find the modern equivalent of a Conestoga wagon almost anywhere, complete with a satellite dish and a patch of Astroturf by the door.

Alas, there are some areas of the state that we really wanted to include but couldn't: Lake Mead, Lake Powell, Lake Havasu, Canyon de Chelly, and the Colorado Corridor, among others. As special as these places are, the campgrounds within them either violated every criterion in this book's subtitle or simply didn't have designated camping that met our standards. (Waterfall-studded Havasu Canyon actually offers *fantastic* tent camping, but because that destination is accessible only by helicopter or an 11-mile hike or horse/mule ride, it didn't make the cut.) Tenters looking for solitude in these areas might want to rent a boat and camp on the shoreline or find a dispersed spot in the surrounding wilderness.

Finally, note that while the various managing agencies work hard to keep their websites and print information accurate and up to date, in updating this edition we found that a few campgrounds from the first edition were closed. It's always a good idea to call the park or ranger district before you go for news on current conditions and unexpected events such as fires and floods.

We hope that *Best Tent Camping: Arizona* will take the legwork out of choosing the campground that's right for you!

THE RATING SYSTEM

As with all books in the Best Tent Camping series, the authors personally experienced dozens of campgrounds and campsites to select the top 50 locations in Arizona. Within that universe of 50 sites, the author then ranked each one according to the six categories described below.

Each campground is superlative in its own way. For example, a site may be rated only one star in one category but perhaps five stars in another category. Our rating system allows you to choose your destination based on the attributes that are most important to you. Although these ratings are subjective, they're still excellent guidelines for finding the perfect camping experience for you and your companions.

Below and following we describe the criteria for each of the attributes in our five-star rating system:

★★★★★   The site is **ideal** in that category.

★★★★   The site is **exemplary** in that category.

★★★   The site is **very good** in that category.

★★   The site is **above average** in that category.

★   The site is **acceptable** in that category.

INDIVIDUAL RATINGS

Each campground description includes ratings for **beauty, privacy, spaciousness, quiet, security,** and **cleanliness;** each attribute is ranked from one to five stars, with five being the best. Yes, these ratings are subjective, but we've tried to select campgrounds that offer something for everyone.

BEAUTY

Beauty, of course, is in the eye of the beholder, but we gave higher marks for panoramic views or proximity to a lake or river. A campground that blended in well with the environment scored well, as did areas with remarkable wildlife or geology. Well-grown vegetation and nicely laid-out sites also upped the ratings.

PRIVACY

For this category we looked at the number of sites, the amount of screening between them, and the physical distance from one site to one another. Other considerations included the presence of nearby trails or day-use areas, along with proximity to a town or city that would invite regular day-use traffic and perhaps compromise privacy.

SPACIOUSNESS

Spaciousness is both a matter of actual space and of the feeling of having elbow room. We checked the separation of tent spots, picnic tables, cooking areas, and vehicles. We adjusted our marks based on whether activity areas and tent pads were defined or bordered and scored higher for the potential to spread out. We also gave campgrounds with plenty of space between the sites a higher rating than more crowded campgrounds.

QUIET

The quietness of a campground of course depends on who your neighbors are and when you're visiting. We took into consideration our experience at the campsite, the nearness of roads, the proximity of towns and cities, the probable number of RVs, the likelihood of noisy all-terrain vehicles or boats, and whether a campground host is available or willing to enforce quiet hours. If we heard that a campground had a reputation for rowdiness or if we heard or witnessed a ruckus ourselves, we removed it from consideration.

Note that some of these campgrounds have no specified quiet hours; nevertheless, you should use common sense and be considerate of others.

SECURITY

Determining a campground's level of security depends on what you view as the greater risk: other people or the wilderness. The more remote the campground, the less likely you are to run into opportunistic crime, but on the downside, the harder it is to get help in case of an accident or confrontation. The security rating takes into consideration whether the campground has a host or resident park ranger, the proximity of other campsites, how much day traffic the campground receives, how close the campground is to a town or city, and whether there is cell coverage or some type of emergency notification.

CLEANLINESS

This often depends on who was camping right before you and how your visit coincides with the campground's maintenance schedule. In general, we gave higher marks to campgrounds with hosts who cleaned up regularly; we also gave high marks in the rare case of odor-free toilets. At unhosted campgrounds, we looked for trash receptacles as well as evidence that sites were cleared and that signs and buildings were kept repaired. We didn't necessarily mark down for a single visitor's garbage left at a site, but we definitely did for trash deposited in shrubbery or along trails, indicating infrequent cleaning.

THE CAMPGROUND PROFILE

Each profile contains a concise but informative narrative of the campground and individual sites. In addition to the property, the recreational opportunities are also described—what's in the area and perhaps suggestions for touristy activities. This descriptive text is enhanced with three helpful elements: **Ratings, Key Information,** and **Getting There** (accurate driving directions that lead you to the campground from the nearest major roadway, along with GPS coordinates).

THE CAMPGROUND LOCATOR MAP AND MAP LEGEND

Use the Arizona Campground Locator Map, opposite the Table of Contents on page iv, to assess the exact location of each campground. The campground's number appears not only on the overview map but also in the table of contents and on the profile's first page.

A map legend that details the symbols found on the campground-layout maps appears immediately following the Table of Contents, on page vii.

CAMPGROUND-LAYOUT MAPS

Each profile includes a detailed map of individual campsites, roads, facilities, and other key elements.

GPS CAMPGROUND-ENTRANCE COORDINATES

Readers can easily access all campgrounds in this book by using the directions given and the overview map, which shows at least one major road leading into the area. But for those who enjoy using GPS technology to navigate, the book includes coordinates for each campground's entrance in latitude and longitude, expressed in degrees and decimal minutes.

To convert GPS coordinates from degrees, minutes, and seconds to degrees and decimal minutes, divide the seconds by 60 (or visit a website such as directionsmag.com/site /latlong-converter). For more information about GPS technology, visit usgs.gov.

A note of caution: A dedicated GPS unit will easily guide you to any of these campgrounds, but users of smartphone mapping apps may find that cell service is often unavailable in the remote areas where many of these hideaways are located.

WEATHER

Many people fear desert creatures such as rattlesnakes and scorpions but will practically flirt with Arizona's biggest danger—the sun. Make no mistake: it gets hot here, and don't let anyone tell you that just because it's a dry heat that it's not so bad.

Dehydration and heat exhaustion commonly afflict the unprepared, the unwary, or the merely overconfident. Carry 3 liters of water per person, per day, and consider investing in a collapsible water container (Camelbak and Platypus make good ones)—making the water you carry more accessible increases the likelihood that you'll actually drink enough of it.

Pro tip: Fill empty 2-liter soda bottles or plastic juice bottles with water, freeze them, and use them in your cooler instead of ice cubes. When the ice melts, you have a backup supply of drinking water, or you can use it to put out your campfire.

Wear a wide-brimmed hat, sunscreen, and sunglasses, along with lightweight long-sleeved shirts and pants if you expect to be in the sun all day. Covering up in the heat may seem counterintuitive, but you'll stay cooler if you protect your skin from the sun.

You shouldn't plan just for the heat, however; you should prepare for cool nights as well—once the sun sets out in the desert, it can get chilly fast. Bring layers and expect the unexpected from Arizona's weather. We've included campgrounds in locations ranging everywhere from 1,700 to 9,000 feet in elevation. You'll experience major changes in temperature, weather, and plant life as you change elevations. Knowing the campground's elevation, listed in each profile's Key Information box, will give you an idea of what conditions to prepare for.

The summer monsoon season lasts from mid-July through early September. Expect heavy afternoon rains nearly every day, and be aware that the rain can sometimes turn to hail at higher elevations. Bring a tarp to cover your gear, and carry a poncho or rain jacket. These pouring rains often fall on soil that's too dry or stony to absorb them, making monsoon season prime flash-flood time. Always place your tent with an eye to drainage and never take chances when trying to cross a flooded wash, no matter how big your vehicle is.

The rainy season is also part of the fire season, as lightning strikes spark many forest fires. Many other fires, sadly, are caused by carelessness. *Always* douse your campfires completely; we carry a 6-gallon jug of water in our truck specifically for that purpose. Keep your campfire under control and below knee level, or better yet, use a gas stove, which does less damage to the ground and roots beneath. Seasonal fire restrictions are no joke, and the penalties for disregarding them are serious.

FIRST AID KIT

A useful first aid kit may contain more items than you might think necessary. These are just the basics. Prepackaged kits in waterproof bags (Atwater Carey and Adventure Medical make them) are available. As a preventive measure, take along sunscreen and insect repellent. Even though quite a few items are listed here, they pack down into a small space:

- Ace bandages or Spenco joint wraps

- Adhesive bandages

- Antibiotic ointment (Neosporin or the generic equivalent)

- Antiseptic or disinfectant, such as Betadine or hydrogen peroxide

- Aspirin, acetaminophen (Tylenol), or ibuprofen (Advil)

- Butterfly-closure bandages

- Comb and tweezers (for removing ticks from your skin)

- Diphenhydramine (Benadryl, in case of allergic reactions)

- Epinephrine (EpiPen) in a prefilled syringe (for severe allergic reactions to outdoor mishaps such as bee stings)

- Gauze (one roll and six 4-by-4-inch compress pads)

- LED flashlight or headlamp

- Matches or lighter

- Moist towelettes

- Moleskin/Spenco 2nd Skin

- Pocketknife or multipurpose tool

- Waterproof first aid tape

- Whistle (for signaling rescuers if you get lost or hurt)

FLORA AND FAUNA PRECAUTIONS

WILD CREATURES

You may be concerned about encountering wildlife such as rattlesnakes, scorpions, black bears, wolves, coyotes, and mountain lions. Be aware, however, that your chances of even glimpsing most of these critters are actually pretty slim—they'll usually go out of their way to avoid you.

Photo: Charles Liu

You will possibly encounter rattlesnakes in any area in this book. Rattlesnakes like to bask in the sun and won't bite unless threatened. However, the snakes you most likely will see while hiking will be nonvenomous species and subspecies. The best rule is to leave all snakes alone, give them a wide berth as you hike past, and make sure any hiking companions (including dogs) do the same. When hiking, stick to well-used trails, and wear over-the-ankle boots and loose-fitting long pants. Do not step or put your hands beyond your range of detailed visibility, and avoid wandering around in the dark. Step *onto* logs and rocks, never *over* them, and be especially careful when climbing rocks. Always avoid walking through dense brush or willow thickets.

Follow these few simple rules to reduce the chance of an up-close-and-personal wild-animal experience:

- **CLEAN UP AFTER YOURSELF IN CAMP.** Store food and toiletries in your vehicle or a bearproof container, or hang them from a tree—don't keep them in your tent.

- **DON'T LEAVE SHOES OR OTHER GEAR** outside of your tent overnight, or be sure to shake them out before using them.

- **KEEP TRACK OF YOUR KIDS**, and leash your pets.

- **DON'T STICK YOUR HANDS AND FEET** into places where you can't see.

If you encounter a wild animal, give it plenty of space, and don't provoke it. You're much more likely to be endangered by elk and deer (and cows) while you're on the road than by bears, mountain lions, and the like. As the four-part warning signs along some of Arizona's highways say: "Elk are large / In herds they run / Across the highway / Don't hit one!"

POISONOUS (AND PAINFUL) PLANTS

Arizona is known for its prickly plants. To protect themselves from predators, many desert plants have spikes and spines instead of leaves. The safest way to avoid a run-in with them is to stay on maintained trails, keep kids in sight, and keep dogs on a leash. Carry a comb to remove such prickly hangers-on as jumping cholla (*right*).

Photo: Kelly Phillips

You may not think of poison ivy as a desert plant, but it's actually quite common in Arizona's riparian habitats. Recognizing poison ivy and avoiding contact with it are the most effective ways to prevent the painful, itchy rashes associated with this plant. Poison

Photo: Kelly Phillips

ivy (*left*) ranges from a thick, tree-hugging vine to a shaded ground cover, 3 leaflets to a leaf. Urushiol, the plant's oily sap, is responsible for the rash. Usually within 12–14 hours of exposure (but sometimes much later), raised lines and/or blisters will appear, accompanied by a terrible itch. Try not to scratch—dirty fingernails can cause an infection, and in the best case you'll spread the rash to other parts of your body.

Wash the rash with cold water and a mild soap or cleanser such as Tecnu, and dry it thoroughly, applying calamine lotion or a topical cortisone cream to help soothe the itch; if the rash is painful or blistering is severe, seek medical attention. Note that any oil that gets on clothing, boots, and the like can keep spreading its misery for at least a year if you don't thoroughly clean it off, so wash everything that you think could have urushiol on it, including pets.

Another plant found in riparian habitats and disturbed sites is poison hemlock (*right*). It has hollow stems, and its toxin is potent enough to kill children who put the stems in their mouths. Hemlock is very close in appearance to Queen Anne's lace—look for the purple-spotted stems to identify this plant and avoiding coming in contact with any part of it.

Photo: William and Wilma Follette/USDA Natural Resources Conservation Service (public domain)

Arizona is also known for hallucinogenic plants such as sacred datura and peyote. Although these plants have long been used in American Indian religious ceremonies, that use comes with wisdom accumulated over centuries. Experimenting on your own will likely cause major illness and possibly death.

Another plant to avoid is black nightshade, a relative of deadly nightshade. Common along roadsides and in disturbed habitats, it has small green, yellow, or black berries that can look appealing to small children.

In general, it's unwise to eat any wild plant unless you have specific knowledge about foraging in Arizona and proper plant-identification skills.

ROADS AND VEHICLES

While doing the research for this book and bumping along dirt roads all over the state, we reset our standards for what constitutes a good road. We consider a good road to be wide, well-graded dirt, with few rocks or dips, enabling us to clip along at 30 mph.

We traveled to the campgrounds in this book in a stock four-wheel-drive Toyota T100 or a Subaru Forester, and after driving 12,000 miles, we've only had to replace the shocks and brakes, tighten a few loose bolts, and fix one flat tire. High clearance gives you the ability to cruise most of the state's back roads, and a 4WD can get you out of a sticky situation, but the majority of these campgrounds can be reached by a careful driver in a standard sedan when the roads are dry. Note that road conditions can change quickly with the weather, so be sure to call 511 or the phone number in the campground entry to get a report on road conditions. Obey all traffic signs, and keep in mind that vehicles driving uphill have the right-of-way on narrow roads.

Arizona's hundreds of miles of Forest Service roads can open a lot of backcountry to those of us who aren't long-distance backpackers. Get a good, detailed paper map, such as the *DeLorme Gazetteer*, if you intend to travel the back roads, make sure your vehicle is in good shape, and carry an emergency kit with plenty of water.

Note that Forest Service roads often close temporarily due to hazards such as fire, flooding, and poor surface conditions, or seasonally due to snow or in order to protect wildlife. It's your responsibility to know which roads are closed, so pick up a free **Motor Vehicle Use Map** at any USFS visitor center or ranger-district office, or download a digital version to your smartphone or GPS. It's also a good idea to check road conditions at the website of the national forest you plan to camp in.

PERMITS AND ACCESS

If, like us, you enjoy exploring Arizona, you might benefit by purchasing an **America the Beautiful National Parks and Federal Recreational Lands Annual Pass,** more concisely known as an **Interagency Pass.** The current cost is $80 per year, which covers entrance to all national parks (including Grand Canyon) and national monuments, as well as most fee areas within lands managed by the USFS, the Bureau of Land Management, and the U.S. Fish and Wildlife Service. Many fee areas on federal lands in Sedona also accept the Interagency Pass in place of the local Red Rock Pass.

While the pass doesn't cover camping fees, we've found it very cost-effective when it comes to entrance fees. Seniors age 62 and older may purchase a **Lifetime Pass** for $80, and people with permanent physical disabilities may obtain a free **Access Pass.** If you have a Lifetime or Access Pass, your camping fees at USFS campgrounds are often discounted by half.

Tonto National Forest, which is home to many of the most heavily used recreation areas near Phoenix, operates under a slightly different pass program. The **Tonto National Forest Discovery Pass** is required at many recreation sites, especially in ranger districts close to Phoenix. Daily passes can be purchased at USFS offices, online, and from local retail stores, but they're usually unavailable for sale at the recreation sites themselves. Check tinyurl.com /tontopasses for a list of vendors.

Each pass has scratch-off date blocks, so you can buy them in advance and mark them on the day of use. Daily Discovery Passes cost $8 per vehicle and $4 per watercraft; annual Discovery Passes cost $80, and annual Senior and Access Discovery Passes cost $60.

Camping at **Arizona State Parks** entitles you to a waiver of a given park's daily entrance fee; for more information, visit azstateparks.com/fee-schedule. The **Arizona State Parks Annual Pass** ($75) is a good deal if you plan to visit several parks a year without camping. Many regional and county parks throughout the state also issue annual passes, but they're park-specific.

You may also want to purchase the $15 **State Land Recreational Permit,** which allows you to hike, camp, or drive off-road on Arizona State Trust lands and is available from the Arizona State Land Department. You won't need this permit to camp at any of the campgrounds in this book, but it wouldn't hurt to have on hand if you plan to drive off-road often. Check land.az.gov for rules and regulations and to download a permit application.

Finally, note that Arizona's **Indian reservations** are self-governing territories with their own rules and regulations for outdoor activities and backcountry travel. If you'd like to spend time on tribal lands, check in with the local authorities for specific information.

HAPPY CAMPING: PLANNING, ETIQUETTE, AND MORE

Few things are more disappointing than a bad camping trip—the good news is, it's really easy to have a great one. Here are a few things to consider as you prepare for your trip:

- **PLAN AHEAD.** Know your equipment, your ability, and the area where you'll be camping—and prepare accordingly. Be self-sufficient at all times; carry the necessary supplies for changes in weather or other conditions.

  In the same vein, reserve your site in advance when that's an option, especially if it's a weekend or holiday or if the campground is extremely popular. Finally, consider the accessibility of supplies before you go—it's a pain to have to get in the car and make a long trek in search of hot dog buns or bug spray.

- **USE CARE WHEN TRAVELING.** Stay on designated roads. Be respectful of private property and travel restrictions. Familiarize yourself with the area you'll be traveling in by picking up a map that shows land ownership.

- **CONSIDER YOUR SPACE REQUIREMENTS.** In general, choose a single site if your group consists of 8 people or fewer, a double site for groups of up to

16 people, a triple site for groups of up to 24, or a group camping area for groups larger than 24.

- **PLAY BY THE RULES.** If you're unhappy with the site you've selected, check with the campground host for other options. Don't just grab a seemingly empty site that looks more appealing than yours—it could be reserved.

- **PICK YOUR CAMPING BUDDIES WISELY.** Make sure that everyone is on the same page regarding expectations of difficulty (amenities or the lack thereof, physical exertion, and so on), sleeping arrangements, and food requirements.

- **DRESS FOR THE SEASON.** Educate yourself on the temperature highs and lows of the specific part of the state you plan to visit. It may be warm at night in the summer in your backyard, but up in the mountains it will be quite chilly.

- **PITCH YOUR TENT ON A LEVEL SURFACE,** preferably one covered with leaves, pine straw, or grass. Use a tarp or specially designed footprint to thwart ground moisture and to protect the tent floor. Before you pitch, do some site cleanup, such as picking up small rocks and sticks that can damage your tent floor and make sleep uncomfortable. If you have a separate rainfly but aren't sure you'll need it, keep it rolled up at the base of your tent in case it starts raining late at night.

- **CONSIDER PACKING A SLEEPING PAD IF THE GROUND MAKES YOU UNCOMFORTABLE.** A wide range of pads in varying sizes and thicknesses is sold at outdoors stores. Inflatable pads are also available; don't try to improvise with a home air mattress, which conducts heat away from the body and tends to deflate as you sleep.

- **DON'T HANG OR TIE CLOTHESLINES, HAMMOCKS, AND EQUIPMENT ON OR TO TREES.** Even if you see other campers doing this, be responsible and do your part to reduce damage to trees and shrubs.

- **IF YOU TEND TO USE THE BATHROOM MULTIPLE TIMES AT NIGHT, PLAN AHEAD.** Leaving a comfy sleeping bag and stumbling around in the dark to find a place to heed nature's call—be it a vault toilet, a full restroom, or just the woods—is no fun. Keep a flashlight and any other accoutrements you may need by the tent door, and know exactly where to head in the dark.

- **WHEN YOU CAMP AT A PRIMITIVE SITE, KNOW HOW TO GO.** Bringing large jugs of water and a portable toilet is the easiest and most environmentally friendly solution. A variety of portable toilets, from plush-seated models to glorified plastic bags, are available from outdoors suppliers; in a pinch, a 5-gallon bucket fitted with a toilet seat and lined with a heavy-duty trash bag will work just as well. (Be sure to pack out the trash bag.)

   A second, less desirable method is to dig a cathole 3–8 inches deep. It should be located at least 200 yards from campsites, trails, and water, in an inconspicuous location with as much undergrowth as possible. Cover the hole with a thin layer of soil after each use, and *don't burn or bury your toilet paper*—pack it out in resealable plastic bags. If you plan to stay at the campsite for several days, dig a new hole each day, being careful to replace the topsoil over the hole from the day before.

In addition to the plastic bags, your outdoor-toilet cache should include a garden trowel, toilet paper, and wet wipes. Select a trowel with a well-designed handle that can also double as a toilet paper dispenser.

- **IF YOU WON'T BE HIKING TO A PRIMITIVE CAMPSITE, DON'T SKIMP ON FOOD.** Plan tasty meals, and bring everything you'll need to prep, cook, eat, and clean up. That said, don't duplicate equipment such as cooking pots among the members of your group.

- **KEEP A CLEAN KITCHEN AREA**, and avoid leaving food scraps on the ground both during and after your visit. Maintain a group trash bag, and be sure to secure it in your vehicle at night. Many sites have a pack-in/pack-out rule, and that means everything: no cheating by tossing orange peels, eggshells, or apple cores in the shrubs.

- **DO YOUR PART TO PREVENT BEARS, RACCOONS, SKUNKS, AND OTHER WILDLIFE FROM BECOMING CONDITIONED TO SEEK HUMAN FOOD.** Store food (including canned goods, soft drinks, and beer) in your vehicle or in animal-proof containers. Keep your garbage secured, and don't take food with you into your tent. You'll also need to stow scented or flavored toiletries such as deodorant, toothpaste, and lip balm, as well as cooking grease and pet food.

  On a related note, an unannounced approach, a sudden movement, or a loud noise will startle any wildlife that happens to wander through the campground. A surprised animal can be dangerous to you, to others, and to itself, so give animals plenty of space.

- **USE ESTABLISHED FIRE RINGS, AND CHECK AHEAD TO FAMILIARIZE YOURSELF WITH ALL RELEVANT FIRE RESTRICTIONS/BANS.** (In Arizona, open fires are usually permitted except during especially dry times and in especially fire-vulnerable areas.) Make sure that your campfire is totally extinguished before you turn in for the night or before you leave your site. Please don't burn your garbage—trash fires smell awful and often don't burn completely, and fire rings fill with unsightly burned litter over time.

  Check ahead to see if bringing your own firewood is allowed. If it's not, buying firewood on-site (if available) may be preferable to gathering deadfall, which can be green and/or wet.

- **DON'T WASH DISHES AND LAUNDRY OR BATHE IN STREAMS AND LAKES.** Food scraps are unsightly and can be potentially harmful to fish, and even biodegradable dish soap can be harmful to fragile aquatic environments.

- **BE A GOOD NEIGHBOR.** Be aware of quiet hours, especially when pulling into a campground after dark. Keep your pets leashed and under control. Avoid shining your headlights or flashlights into other campsites as you search for a spot. And please turn down your car stereo—that bass beat carries farther than you think.

    In addition, walk on designated paths and roads, and respect the privacy of your neighbors by not strolling through their sites to get to the restrooms. You'll also reduce damage to the foliage and keep the campground green by sticking to the main trail.

- **MOST OF ALL, LEAVE YOUR CAMP CLEANER THAN YOU FOUND IT.** In Girl Scouts, we were taught to scavenge around the campsite picking up every piece of trash we could find, even if it wasn't ours. Make cleaning up into a game with your kids: whoever packs out the most twist ties, pop tops, and gum wrappers is the winner.

VENTURING AWAY FROM THE CAMPGROUND

If you decide to go for a hike, bike, or other excursion off-site, here are some safety tips.

- **LET SOMEONE AT HOME OR AT CAMP KNOW WHERE YOU'LL BE GOING AND HOW LONG YOU EXPECT TO BE GONE.** This can be a lifesaver if something untoward happens, and it also keeps your loved ones from worrying. We're in the habit of sending Kirstin's sister a text message once we decide where we we're going to camp and then checking in when we arrive home.

- **SIGN IN AND OUT OF ANY TRAIL REGISTERS PROVIDED.** Leave notes on trail conditions if space allows—that's your opportunity to alert others to any problems you encounter.

- **DON'T ASSUME THAT YOUR PHONE WILL WORK ON THE TRAIL.** Reception may be spotty or nonexistent, especially on a trail embraced by towering trees.

- **ALWAYS CARRY FOOD AND WATER, EVEN FOR A SHORT HIKE.** We recommend a minimum of 3 liters of water per person, per day. If you're used to depending on water from lakes or streams, remember that most of Arizona's few water sources are ephemeral and, when present, are frequently shared with livestock. Always treat so-called found water by boiling, filtering, or chemically treating it before drinking.

- **ASK QUESTIONS.** Public-land employees are on hand to help.

- **STAY ON DESIGNATED TRAILS.** If you become disoriented, assess your current direction, and then retrace your steps to the point where you went astray. Using a map, compass, and/or GPS unit, and keeping in mind what you've passed thus far, reorient yourself and trust your judgment on which way to continue. If you become absolutely unsure of how to continue, return to your vehicle the way you came in. Should you become completely lost, remaining in place and waiting for help is most often the best option for adults and always the best option for children.

- **CARRY A WHISTLE.** It could save your life if you get lost or injured.

- **BE ESPECIALLY CAREFUL WHEN CROSSING STREAMS.** Whether you're fording a stream or crossing on a log, make every step count. If you have any doubt about maintaining your balance on a log, ford the stream instead: use a trekking pole or stout stick for balance and *face upstream as you cross.* If a stream seems too deep to ford, turn back.

- **BE CAREFUL AT OVERLOOKS.** While these areas provide spectacular views, they're also potentially hazardous. Stay back from the edge of outcrops, and be absolutely sure of your footing.

- **STANDING DEAD TREES AND STORM-DAMAGED LIVING TREES CAN POSE A REAL HAZARD TO TENT CAMPERS.** These trees may have loose or broken limbs that could fall at any time. When choosing a campsite or just a spot to rest during a hike, *look up*—this is an especially important precaution in Arizona's many fire-damaged areas.

- **KNOW THE SYMPTOMS OF ABNORMALLY HIGH BODY TEMPERATURE, OR HYPERTHERMIA.** Lightheadedness and weakness are the first two indicators. If you feel these symptoms, find some shade, drink some water, remove as many layers of clothing as practical, and stay put until you cool down. Marching through heat exhaustion leads to heatstroke—which can be fatal. If you should be sweating and you're not, that's the signature warning sign. If you or a hiking partner is experiencing heatstroke, do whatever you can to get cool and find help.

- **LIKEWISE, KNOW THE SYMPTOMS OF SUBNORMAL BODY TEMPERATURE, OR HYPOTHERMIA.** Shivering and forgetfulness are the two most common indicators. Hypothermia can occur at any elevation, even in the summer—especially if you're wearing lightweight cotton clothing. If symptoms develop, get to shelter, hot liquids, and dry clothes as soon as possible.

- **MOST IMPORTANT, TAKE ALONG YOUR BRAIN.** Think before you act. Watch your step. Plan ahead.

Now that your windshield is decked out in passes and your head is full of facts, take this handy book and get out there. The best tent camping in Arizona is waiting for you!

NORTHERN ARIZONA

An iconic vista of Monument Valley from The View Campground (campground 9, page 39)

1

⛺ Canyon View Campground

Beauty ★★★★ Privacy ★★★ Spaciousness ★★★ Quiet ★★★★★ Security ★★★★ Cleanliness ★★★★★

Navajo National Monument is home to some of the best-preserved cliff dwellings in the country.

The Navajo Nation is best known for the austere beauty of the Painted Desert, with its rough, red mountains and color-striped mineral badlands, and the stark magnificence of Monument Valley. Between the two, a surprise awaits in the pinyon-brushed hills near Kayenta—the lovely gem of Navajo National Monument. Established in 1909 and managed by the National Park Service, it protects three Ancestral Puebloan ruins—Betatakin, Keet Seel, and Inscription House. Built in the 13th century by the Hisatsinom, ancient ancestors of today's Hopi clans, these are among the best-preserved cliff dwellings in the country, and remain culturally important for the Hopi, Zuni, Paiute, and Diné (Navajo) peoples.

When you first enter the park, stop at the visitor center to chat with the rangers, many of whom are Diné, and see the interpretive displays and ancient pottery. Artisans frequently demonstrate traditional crafts such as rug weaving, and next door you'll find a gift shop specializing in silver Navajo jewelry. The visitor center also offers flush toilets, drinking fountains, and a picnic area. You can crawl into the nearby sweathouse and imagine what it was like to bathe without water and dry off with sand. Stand in the hogan, an example of traditional Navajo housing, then head out to pitch your own tent.

Looking east toward Tsegi Canyon

KEY INFORMATION

CONTACT: 928-672-2700, nps.gov/nava

OPEN: April–September

SITES: 14

EACH SITE HAS: Picnic table, upright grill

ASSIGNMENT: First-come, first-served; reservations not required except for groups of 10 or more (contact the campground for details)

REGISTRATION: Not required

AMENITIES: Vault toilets, group sites

PARKING: At campsites

FEE: None; donations accepted

ELEVATION: 7,300'

RESTRICTIONS:

PETS: On leash only; not allowed on trails

FIRES: No wood fires

ALCOHOL: Prohibited

VEHICLES: 28-foot length limit

QUIET HOURS: 10 p.m.–6 a.m.

OTHER: 7-day stay limit/calendar year; firearms prohibited

With two no-fee campgrounds at the monument, you can choose the amenities that best suit you. Sunset View Campground provides paved roads and parking tabs, wheelchair-accessible spots, flush toilets, a service sink and gray water disposal, and, of course, views of the setting sun. We recommend Canyon View, designed for tent campers who prefer a simpler, more secluded experience. Take a right as you leave the visitor center parking lot, toward the Keet Seel Trail. As you leave the pavement behind you, look for the employee housing on the left and the corral on the right. The Keet Seel Trailhead parking area is just below the entrance to the campground.

A slender thread of sites, Canyon View sits on a ridge between Tsegi Canyon and Shonto Plateau, and almost all of the sites do indeed command a canyon view. You'll find only patchy shade in the pinyon–juniper woodland, but at nearly 7,300 feet elevation, the mornings and evenings prove to be cool and comfortable. Most of the sites are well screened. The first site is very private and set apart with a generous pull-through. Site 2 has a shallower pulloff but offers good morning shade, as do all of the sites on the east side of the road. Sites 7–9, 12, and 13 provide the best view of Betatakin Canyon. Sites 10 and 11 are group sites, available for free on a first-come, first-served basis. Situated in the center of the loop at the end of the line of campsites, site 11 is open and uncomfortably rocky. A large group here would affect sites 9, 12, and 13, which are otherwise quite nice. Site 10 is the better group site, being off to the side with a large, smooth area for tents.

While you won't have a campground host, park employees live nearby. The campgrounds are rarely full—in fact, Canyon View closes during the off-season because of lack of use. If you come when only Sunset View is open, check out site 7, which is below the road and has a nice tent spot; site 15, which is very private at the price of a little hill climb; or site 16, which is nicely screened. The weather can turn cold and snowy in the winter, and no open campfires are permitted in either campground.

During the summer, the Park Service offers daily, free ranger-led hikes to the 125-room alcove at Betatakin (ledge house, also known as *Talastima* in Hopi). Allow three to five hours for this 5-mile round-trip hike. The less ambitious can spot Betatakin from the overlook 0.5 mile down the paved Sandal Trail. Along the path, interpretive signs teach you the names and traditional uses of Navajo and Hopi native plants. An additional 0.8 mile down the steep Aspen Trail allows you a glimpse into a rare pocket of forest lush with aspen and Douglas-fir. If you're up for a longer hike or even a backpack trip, sign up for the 17-mile round-trip hike to Keet Seel (broken pottery, *Kawestima* in Hopi), the largest and longest inhabited of the ruins. The hike requires a backcountry permit, which is free at the visitor center. Only 20 people per day can hike to Keet Seel, so you should make reservations. The path brings you down to the riverbed, with 32 stream crossings and an occasional waterfall along the way. While you can do this as a day hike, you might prefer to backpack in and camp overnight in grasses and trees 0.25 mile from Keet Seel. At the ruin, a ranger guides you up a tall ladder and into the past, five people at a time. Inscription House (*Tsu'ovi*), the most fragile of the three, is closed to visitors.

Canyon View Campground

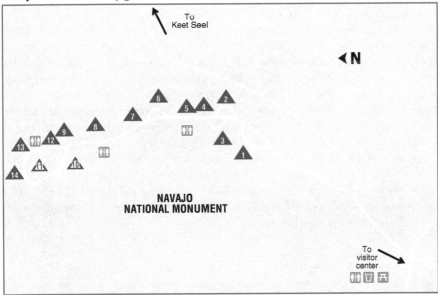

GETTING THERE

From Kayenta, take US 160 southwest 21 miles to AZ 564. Turn right and drive north 9 miles to the Navajo National Monument Visitor Center. Past the visitor center parking lot, turn right at the fork and drive 0.5 mile to Canyon View Campground.

GPS COORDINATES N36° 40.977' W110° 32.548'

2

⛺ Desert View Campground

Beauty ★★★ Privacy ★★★ Spaciousness ★★★ Quiet ★★★ Security ★★★★ Cleanliness ★★★★★

This is the campground to go to if you're looking for a quieter experience at one of the world's largest tourist attractions.

No book about the best camping in Arizona would be complete without mentioning Grand Canyon National Park (thrice, in our case). One of the seven natural wonders of the world, it is Arizona's main claim to fame and receives six million visitors each year. That can mean a lot of chaos and congestion. Luckily, most of those people concentrate near Grand Canyon Village on the South Rim and don't explore the rest of the park. You can still have a peaceful experience at one of the world's largest tourist attractions.

The South Rim offers two developed campgrounds—Mather and Desert View. Mather's 320 campsites are near Grand Canyon Village, the South Rim's hub, with everything you could possibly need. It's open year-round, and reservations are strongly recommended from March 1 through mid-November. Desert View, open seasonally on a first-come first-served basis, is the campground to go to if you are looking for something quieter.

Approaching from the village along Desert View Drive, you pass some of the park's most famous viewpoints, while the flora changes from tall pines to open pinyon–juniper woodland. You won't see the canyon from the campground, but just a short distance away is Desert View Point, site of the Watchtower. Climb to the top, the highest point on the South Rim, for incredible views. The tower itself is a historical landmark, a Pueblo-inspired creation of the Fred Harvey Company's remarkable architect, Mary Jane Elizabeth Colter. You'll also find a gas station, convenience store, snack bar, and gift shop here; close by are the ranger station and the east entrance to the park.

The Grand Canyon from the South Rim

KEY INFORMATION

CONTACT: 928-638-7888, nps.gov/grca

OPEN: Mid-April–mid-October

SITES: 50

EACH SITE HAS: Picnic table, fire ring

ASSIGNMENT: First-come, first-served; no reservations

REGISTRATION: On-site with credit card at automated fee station

AMENITIES: Flush toilets, water spigots, trash, recycling, campground host; gas and general store nearby

PARKING: At campsites

FEE: $12/night, plus $35/week park-entrance fee

ELEVATION: 7,463'

RESTRICTIONS:

PETS: On leash only; prohibited below rim, in park lodging, or on park buses. There is a kennel at South Rim, reservations recommended. Pets are prohibited on North Rim trails.

FIRES: In fire rings only

ALCOHOL: Permitted

VEHICLES: 30-foot length limit; ATVs prohibited; 2-vehicle or 1-RV/trailer limit

QUIET HOURS: 10 p.m.–6 a.m.

OTHER: 7-day stay limit; bear-country food-storage restrictions; firearms prohibited; 6-person limit/site; 2-tent limit; checkout 11 a.m.; no firewood gathering; mountain lion country

In the campground, 50 sites line one long, narrow, paved loop. The sites inside the loop back up to each other, so you don't have much privacy, but the sites on the outside of the loop are more spacious. The junipers and other low scrub provide some screening between most sites, and all of them have a cleared tent area. We think the better sites, inside and out, are on the second half of the loop. Sites 22, 42, and 44 have particularly good screening and separation from their neighbors, and site 29 is spacious and shady, set well back from a generous pullout. The most private site in the campground, and the best choice for summer, is site 46. It's small, but has a complete screen of junipers and a deeply shaded tent spot.

Ravens keep a close eye on you in camp, and if you turn your back, the swoosh of big, black wings will signal the disappearance of anything that looks like food. Given enough time, a Grand Canyon raven will even unzip a backpack and rifle through it. For your sake and theirs, keep a tidy camp kitchen and store your food well.

Large RVs are encouraged to stay at Trailer Village, but smaller RVs, often rentals, are everywhere. The park has set longer quiet hours than you'll find in many campgrounds: generator use is limited to 8 a.m.–8 p.m., and loud music is prohibited at all times. Your fellow campers may come from all over the globe, so say hi and enjoy meeting someone new and different.

The best way to enjoy your visit to the Grand Canyon is to plan ahead. Peruse the National Park Service website and call the information centers. Study up, especially if you intend to enter the canyon itself. Below the rim, the canyon is a uniquely rewarding and uniquely dangerous place to hike. You descend while you're fresh and rested, and only when you're already tired do you face the reality of climbing back up. Throw in the dry, desert climate and the 20°–40° difference between rim and canyon temperatures, and you have a recipe for hundreds of rescues and several deaths every year.

With a little extra planning and effort, you might have a campsite with a view of the canyon all to yourself. You must have a permit to camp outside of designated campgrounds, but backcountry camping can be found both above and below the rim. If you're up for a backpack experience, but don't want to challenge the canyon itself, try Cape Solitude. At-large camping is permitted almost anywhere along the 15.6-mile hike. To explore other possibilities, stop in at the backcountry office, and the rangers will help you plan your ideal trip. Dispersed camping is also available at no cost in Kaibab National Forest, south of the park border.

Don't ignore the most popular parts of the park—the park service has worked hard to make visiting an enjoyable experience, and the lodges and shops at the village have history and charms of their own to explore. A nice way to see the busiest part of the canyon is from the partially paved Rim Trail, which stretches from Hermit's Rest in the west to Yaki Point. You can park at one of the viewpoints, walk all or a portion of the trail, and catch the shuttle bus back to your car. The free, alternative-fuel shuttles don't come as far as Desert View, but if you've come to the canyon via the Grand Canyon Railway (for more details see profile 10, White Horse Lake, page 42), there is taxi service from the village.

Desert View Campground

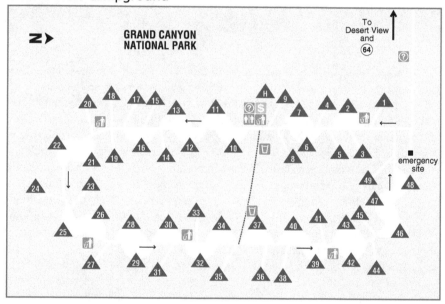

GETTING THERE

From Flagstaff to the east entrance station, take US 89 north 65 miles to AZ 64. Turn left and drive west 50 miles to Grand Canyon National Park's East Entrance. Turn right into the campground.

From Flagstaff to Grand Canyon Village, take US 180 west 51 miles to AZ 64. Turn right and drive north 31 miles to Grand Canyon National Park's South Rim Entrance.

GPS COORDINATES N36° 02.458' W111° 49.583'

3

Forked Pine Campground

Beauty ★★★★ Privacy ★★★ Spaciousness ★★★ Quiet ★★★ Security ★★★ Cleanliness ★★★

If you intend to fish or would like to wake up to the sun rising over the lake, there's no need to go any farther.

As the temperatures in the desert valleys creep up into the triple digits, people start flocking to Arizona's high country. The Mormon Lake area is a popular summer retreat, with many small lakes and several good campgrounds along scenic Lake Mary Road south from Flagstaff toward Payson. Our favorite of these is Ashurst Lake, a little gem in the pinyon–juniper grasslands. If you intend to fish or would like to wake up to the sun rising over the lake, no need to go any farther.

The route from Flagstaff takes you past Upper Lake Mary, a popular spot for boating, waterskiing, fishing, and bird-watching. Past Lakeview Campground at the intersection with Pine Grove Campground, turn east onto Forest Road 82E, a well-graded dirt road that carries you onto higher ground, passing through large, grassy meadows speckled with ponderosa pines and a few oaks. Look northwest to see the San Francisco Peaks rising over the trees in the distance. This good grazing land borders the Anderson Mesa Wildlife Protection Area, so keep an eye out for elk, mule deer, and pronghorn antelope, as well as cattle.

The San Francisco Peaks peek above the horizon across Ashurst Lake.

KEY INFORMATION

CONTACT: 928-526-0866, tinyurl.com
/forkedpine

OPEN: Year-round when roads are open;
full services mid-May–October 1

SITES: 24

EACH SITE HAS: Picnic table, fire ring
with grill

ASSIGNMENT: First-come, first-served;
no reservations

REGISTRATION: With camp host

AMENITIES: Vault toilets, firewood, boat
ramp, campground host, day-use area

PARKING: At campsites

FEE: $18/night, $8/additional vehicle,
$8 day use

ELEVATION: 7,132'

RESTRICTIONS:

PETS: On leash only

FIRES: In fire rings only

ALCOHOL: Permitted

VEHICLES: 35-foot length limit; 1 vehicle
/site; motorbikes restricted to entering
and exiting campsite

QUIET HOURS: 10 p.m.–6 a.m.

OTHER: 14-day stay limit; 8-person limit/site;
10-horsepower boat-motor size limit;
horses prohibited

As you pull up to Ashurst Lake, take a left at the fork in the road and drive around the lake to Forked Pine Campground. Here you will find 24 sites in three loops, with views of the lake and the San Francisco Peaks in the background. All sites contain a picnic table and a steel fire ring with a grill, and most have a cleared, leveled tent area. In loop A, the campground hosts who live here from mid-May through the end of September take site number 6. Of the eight sites here, check out open sites 7 and 8, nearest to the lake, or site 3, tucked in between the shelter of junipers but with less of a lake view. If you prefer more privacy, we recommend heading on to loop B's four sites, where sites 12 and 13 sit near the water's edge for convenient kayak access. There is no toilet facility in this loop, so you will have to take the short walk to loop C to answer the call of nature. Loop C is the largest loop with 12 sites, several with convenient access to the lake for fishing and water play. If the wind is blowing, try small but sheltered site 18; for sunshine and a wide-open feeling, look at lakeside sites 22 and 23. You are also close to the bouldery boat ramp here, near site 20.

Man-made Ashurst Lake was dammed in 1954 to provide water for recreational fishing. The 230-acre lake is frequently stocked with trout, bass, and channel catfish, so bring your fishing pole and canoe or small boat (as long as the motor is less than 10 horsepower). Anderson Mesa has been designated an Important Bird Area—come here for great birdwatching, particularly during migrations. If you should see an osprey drop from the sky and splash up with a fish, look for the bird to turn the catch in its talons in flight so that it faces aerodynamically forward. Among the coots (the lake's most common denizens in every season), look for pied-billed grebes, whose telltale sign is the uncanny ability to duck underwater as soon as you get your binoculars pointed in their direction. During spring and fall migration, you may see northern shovelers, cinnamon teals, northern pintails and ring-necked ducks, plus western grebes courting with their long, swanlike necks. Mountain bluebirds are everywhere, and in the early-morning hours you won't be able to miss the cascading, liquid call of the meadowlark. You may also see less attractive fliers; bring bug spray for spring's no-see-um gnats. Hunters and avid fishermen can use the campground in the off-season, without the comfort of facilities, although in bad winter weather the road may be closed. You're on high, flat land up here, so come prepared for heavy winds in any season.

If you get sick of your camp cooking, head over to Mormon Lake Lodge at Mormon Lake Village. The lodge, open since 1924, has a restaurant and a general store. A catastrophic fire burned the original lodge to the ground in 1974, but local ranchers rebuilt it, and the interior walls still display their cattle brands. Western literature buffs will find a nice selection of Zane Grey memorabilia, as well as a plethora of game trophies. The village also offers gasoline, riding stables, rental cabins, and winter recreation, including snowmobile and cross-country ski rentals.

Mormon Lake is Arizona's largest natural lake, but don't expect much fishing here, as it's often nearly dry. The resulting marshy pasture is a great place to view wildlife, so stop at the overlook and see if you can spot a bald eagle flying overhead, or elk grazing on the tall grasses. One (possibly tall) tale we've been told is that as many as 50 elk will gather in the middle of the lake bed during hunting season, as if some instinct tells them that no hunter will take a shot in the face of an impossibly soggy retrieval.

Forked Pine Campground

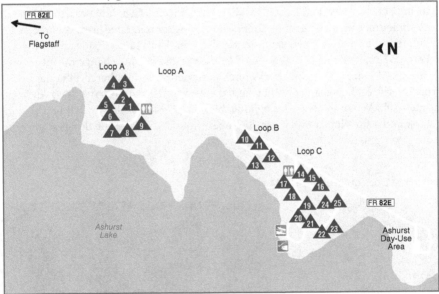

GETTING THERE

From Flagstaff, take Lake Mary Road (FR 3) southeast 17 miles to FR 82E. Turn left and drive east 4 miles to the campground.

GPS COORDINATES N35° 01.372' W111° 23.828'

4

⛺ Freidlein Prairie Dispersed Camping

Beauty ★★★★ Privacy ★★★ Spaciousness ★★★★ Quiet ★★★★ Security ★★★ Cleanliness ★★★★

This campground borders a stand of aspens overlooking a grassy meadow.

Freidlein Prairie Road (Forest Road 522) climbs along the southern flank of the San Francisco Mountains above Flagstaff, through a dense mixed conifer–aspen forest dotted with small clearings. Freidlein Prairie itself (sometimes spelled *Friedlein* or even *Friedlund*) is an irregular patch of aspen-rimmed grassland that, especially in fall when the trees blaze with gold, can easily be seen from town. Wildflowers abound in season, and elk and mule deer graze here throughout the year. This beautiful spot in Coconino National Forest may have been named for an Arizona pioneer family: in 1894, the local newspaper mentioned the theft of a horse from the Friedlein brothers, as well as one Will Friedlein's successful duck-hunting trip to Mormon Lake.

Dispersed camping is allowed through most of Arizona's national forests, providing some of the state's most beautiful and serene camping experiences. In areas of very heavy human impact, such as the Flagstaff wildland-urban interface, however, the U.S. Forest Service sometimes uses "designated dispersed" campsites to reduce fire risk and damage to the land. In 2001 an abandoned campfire off the Freidlein Prairie Road started the 1,300-acre Leroux Fire, spurring the creation of 14 designated sites, a change meant to protect both the fragile forest and your backwoods experience. A numbered fiberglass post by the road marks each site, and another sign, CAMP WITHIN 50' OF THIS POST, defines the campsite itself. While there are no picnic tables or portable toilets, you'll find parking, a tent area, and a fire ring at every site. The beginning and end of the designated camping area are also signed.

Aspens lend a touch of fall gold to site 14.

KEY INFORMATION

CONTACT: 928-526-0866, tinyurl.com
/freidleinprairie

OPEN: Year-round; sites 10–14 closed
March 1–August 31

SITES: 14

EACH SITE HAS: Fire ring

ASSIGNMENT: First-come, first-served;
no reservations

REGISTRATION: Not required

AMENITIES: None

PARKING: At campsites

FEE: None

ELEVATION: 7,900'–8,600'

RESTRICTIONS:

PETS: On leash only

FIRES: In fire rings only

ALCOHOL: Permitted

VEHICLES: RVs and trailers not
recommended; motorized/mechanized
vehicles not permitted in the Kachina
Peaks Wilderness.

QUIET HOURS: Not specified

OTHER: 14-day stay limit; pack in/pack out;
no drinking water available; bear-country
food-storage restrictions

The first two sites are fairly close to FR 516, also known as the Snowbowl Road. If you don't want to go too far up the rugged road to get to the remaining sites, site 3 has a nice, open feeling. Sites 4 and 5 are neighborly, but not on top of each other; sites 6 and 7 should appeal to two groups camping together, since they're just separated by a small mound of boulders. While Freidlein Prairie Road is definitely unimproved, passenger cars with good ground clearance should be able to make it at least as far as site 7 in dry weather.

Sites 8 and 9 sit off 9002W, a spur road to the south. Wildlife spotting should be terrific from site 8, which sits at the ferny border of a stand of aspens overlooking a grassy meadow. Site 9 is among ponderosa pines at the very edge of the designated camping area. It's close to the road, but you'll see more saucy Steller's jays than passing vehicles on this dead end.

Back on the main road, the landscape gets rockier. Freidlein Prairie is actually a well-known bouldering spot, with at least one published guide to the best climbs. It's a few minutes' drive to reach shallow site 10. Site 11 is on a ledge below the road, surrounded by boulders. Sites 12 and 13 are nice, but our pick for beauty is site 14, a tight spot among lichen-covered boulders and bright-green ferns. Note that sites 10–14 are closed March 1–August 31, the nesting season of the Mexican spotted owl. Any traditional nesting area may be important to the survival of this endangered species, so please respect the closure.

With no services available in the Freidlein Prairie area, pack-in/pack-out and Leave No Trace practices are required. With any luck, the camper before you had good wilderness ethics, but if not, remember that an extra trash bag and five generous minutes on your part can transform a campsite for yourself and those who follow you. Keep in mind this is bear country, so be bear safe.

Elevation along the road ranges from 7,900 to 8,600 feet, with cool summer days and the possibility of cold nights. You're near Arizona Snowbowl here, one of the state's prime downhill-ski areas, as well as the Arizona Nordic Village, so expect wintry weather anytime from early fall to late spring. In the winter, Snowbowl maintains FR 516—the primary access to Freidlein Prairie Road—but the ski area's personnel only plow when Snowbowl is open. If you're truly hardy and ready to try winter camping here, check the Snowbowl and Coconino National Forest websites to assess conditions. You'll need a free winter backcountry permit (available at the ski area if open or from the Flagstaff Ranger Station) for winter camping and snow play in the Kachina Peaks Wilderness area.

You can find summer fun at Snowbowl as well, with daily scenic lift rides up Agassiz Peak and ranger talks at the top. Have a deli-style lunch at the Agassiz Lodge Restaurant, then head out for a hike. You can use Snowbowl as the jumping-off point for some great hikes in the Kachina Peaks Wilderness, including a 4.5-mile, 3,300-foot climb to the top of Humphreys Peak (Arizona's highest at 12,633') and the Kachina Trail, a more moderate 7-mile ramble across the slopes of the ancient volcano, which terminates at the end of FR 522.

For more information about Flagstaff's charms and area attractions, see the next profile, Lockett Meadow Campground.

Freidlein Prairie Dispersed Camping

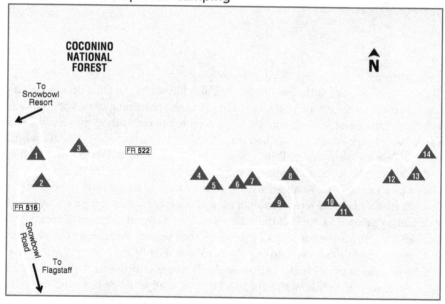

GETTING THERE

From Flagstaff, take US 180 northwest 7.4 miles to Snowbowl Road; then turn right and drive north 2.4 miles to FR 522. Turn right into the dispersed area.

GPS COORDINATES N35° 17.473' W111° 42.403'

5

Lockett Meadow Campground

Beauty ★★★★★ Privacy ★★★★ Spaciousness ★★★★ Quiet ★★★★ Security ★★★★ Cleanliness ★★★★★

In spring and summer, the meadow is spangled with wildflowers, and in late September and early October, the changing aspens splash the mountainsides with bright gold.

Approaching Flagstaff from any direction, the first thing you'll notice is the San Francisco Peaks. Volcanic upheaval created this range, and after a million years of erosion, these are still Arizona's highest mountains. For centuries the peaks, frequently snowcapped or shrouded in rain clouds, have held spiritual significance for Native Americans. They form the Sacred Mountain of the West and the boundary of the Navajo Nation; they're also visible from the mesas of the Hopi, who believe that the Kachina spirits call these mountains home. The Kachina Peaks Wilderness encompasses the heart of this ancient volcano.

On the edge of this wilderness, nestled high on the eastern slopes, is the alpine haven of Lockett Meadow Campground. The narrow unpaved road winds up the mountain, revealing magnificent views past the cinder cones and lava fields of Sunset Crater National Monument and out to the Painted Desert. This challenging route is usually passable by passenger cars in dry weather but is definitely not recommended for RVs or trailers. At its end, towering Douglas-fir, ponderosa pines, and quaking aspens surround several acres of upland prairie grasses, once summer grazing for the sheep of homesteader Henry Claiborne Lockett. In spring and summer, the meadow is spangled with wildflowers, and in late September and early October, the changing aspens splash the mountainsides with bright gold. Stand

Volcanic peaks around the Inner Basin form the backdrop for Lockett Meadow.

KEY INFORMATION

CONTACT: 928-526-0866, tinyurl.com
/lockettmeadow

OPEN: Mid-May–mid-October

SITES: 17

EACH SITE HAS: Picnic table, fire ring

ASSIGNMENT: First-come, first-served;
no reservations

REGISTRATION: Self-register on-site

AMENITIES: Vault toilets

PARKING: At campsites, at trailhead

FEE: $16/night, $8/additional vehicle,
$8 day use

ELEVATION: 8,600'

RESTRICTIONS:

PETS: On leash only

FIRES: In fire rings only

ALCOHOL: Permitted

VEHICLES: RVs and trailers not
recommended; 2 vehicles/site; ATVs
or motorbikes prohibited except to
and from campground; mountain
bikes prohibited in wilderness

QUIET HOURS: 10 p.m.–6 a.m.

OTHER: 14-day stay limit; 8-person limit/site;
bear-country food-storage restrictions;
firearms prohibited; horses prohibited

quietly at sunrise or sunset and you may see foraging elk, mule deer, porcupine, or even a black bear. Listen for voices of the numerous native and migratory birds. The variety of plant and animal life found in these mountains inspired pioneering biologist C. Hart Merriam to develop the ecological concept of life zones.

Lockett Meadow is the only campground this high in the peaks, and it's best to arrive early—the 17 campsites cannot be reserved, and dispersed camping is not permitted near the meadow. The high elevation means you'll enjoy comfortable temperatures all summer, but come prepared for chilly evenings and quickly changing mountain weather in any season. The road is closed in the winter and the campground is unmaintained from October to May, but hardy souls on skis or snowshoes are welcome to use the campsites.

As you reach the campground, the road becomes one-way. The meadow itself is protected grassland closed to camping and vehicles. The campsites are outside the loop, nestled under a canopy of pale aspens and mature ponderosa pines with their vanilla-scented bark. Each site has a picnic table and a fire ring; in dry Arizona it's always a good idea to check with the U.S. Forest Service about fire restrictions. Pull in to the self-service pay station and check out site 1; it's close but nicely screened from the road, and one of the two wildlife watering holes is just through the trees. Our favorite sites are near the busy trailhead, but once the day-use traffic is gone, site 7 may be the most secluded in the campground. Campsites 9–11 provide more room for larger groups, but are also more open to the road and each other. The best views of the meadow and the second pond are from sites 13–16. Two sets of vault toilets serve the campground; there are no other facilities and no drinking water. You won't have a host, but the campground feels fairly secure. Although popular, Lockett Meadow still leaves you with an impression of remoteness and serenity once you're in camp.

The Inner Basin Trail begins its steady uphill climb at Lockett Meadow Campground. The wide, even trail makes a pleasant 3.9-mile round-trip through the forest of the caldera. You'll top 10,000 feet, so be aware of your conditioning and pace yourself. If you're very ambitious, follow the Weatherford Trail to the Humphreys Trail, which takes you to

Arizona's highest point (12,634'). On a clear day you may see all the way to the North Rim of the Grand Canyon. If you have less time or stamina, you can also reach Humphreys Peak by a shorter route from the Snowbowl ski area. Don't be ashamed if acclimated Flagstaff residents jog past you twice while you're still toiling up the trail. From the inner basin you can also access the strenuous Abineau–Bear Jaw Loop hike, which is equally lovely but much less popular. Most of the trail system is in the Kachina Peaks Wilderness, and mountain bikes are not permitted in the fragile alpine environment. Horses, dogs, and camping are also forbidden in the inner basin to protect the mountain aquifer.

Outside the wilderness boundary, Flagstaff is a thriving community rich in natural and human history. Recreational options for all tastes and seasons include downhill and cross-country skiing at Snowbowl and the Arizona Nordic Village, plus plenty of mountain biking in the Coconino National Forest. Crawl through Lava River Cave for an intimate experience of volcanic geology, or stand on the doorstep of history at the ancient pueblos of Wupatki National Monument. Peer into the heavens during a star party at Lowell Observatory, originally built to map the illusory canals of Mars. Learn more about the wonders of the Colorado Plateau at the Museum of Northern Arizona. Or just sit back beneath the aspens in Lockett Meadow and take it easy.

Lockett Meadow Campground

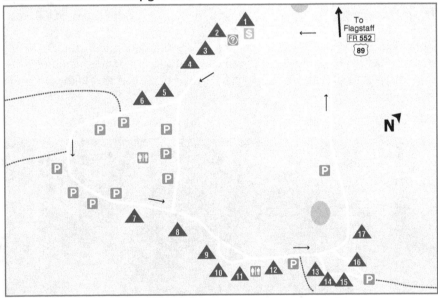

GETTING THERE

From Flagstaff, take US 89 northeast about 12 miles. Turn left onto an unsigned road about 0.1 mile past the FOREST ACCESS sign that's directly across from the SUNSET CRATER NATIONAL MONUMENT sign. Continue approximately 0.5 mile to the signed intersection, and turn right on FR 552. Follow the signs to the campground.

GPS COORDINATES N35° 21.638' W111° 37.187'

6

⚠ Manzanita Campground

Beauty ★★★★ Privacy ★★ Spaciousness ★★★ Quiet ★★★ Security ★★★★ Cleanliness ★★★★★

Perennial Oak Creek has carved this narrow, verdant passage that provides a beautiful setting for fishing, swimming, hiking, or just relaxing.

Sedona has sometimes been called the most beautiful place in the United States. The distinctive red-rock mountains create whimsical shapes that have been named whatever the imagination sees in them—Coffeepot, Snoopy, Cathedral, and Bell. Many believe that these mountains contain vortexes of ethereal energy, and both artists and new agers flock here. You can stroll through the many art galleries, get your tarot cards read, have a past-life regression, or join a vortex hiking tour. Upscale boutiques rub shoulders with shops selling everything from Harley gear to healing crystals.

The stunning scenery makes for a variety of great outdoor experiences. Hike in the serene Secret Mountain Wilderness, bounce around on a guided Pink Jeep tour, or watch the sunset from your resort balcony. One of Sedona's major draws is Oak Creek Canyon. The perennial creek has carved this narrow, verdant passage that provides a beautiful setting for fishing, swimming, hiking, or just relaxing. Just one caveat—this is an extraordinarily popular area, and you'll have the best experience if you come prepared to be patient with your fellow humans.

Of the four campgrounds along Oak Creek Canyon, Manzanita is the closest to the water. Because of its popularity, try to make a reservation ahead of time online or by phone. That way, you're not only guaranteed a spot, it'll be one of the best sites in the campground;

Trees lean toward Oak Creek's cool waters.

KEY INFORMATION

CONTACT: 928-203-7500, tinyurl.com
/manzanitacampground; reservations:
877-444-6777, recreation.gov

OPEN: Year-round

SITES: 18

EACH SITE HAS: Picnic table, fire ring

ASSIGNMENT: First-come, first-served;
reservations available for sites 9, 10, and
12–19 at least 2 days in advance

REGISTRATION: With camp host, on-site,
or online

AMENITIES: Vault toilets, water spigots,
campground host, firewood

PARKING: At campsites

FEE: $22/night; $10 online-reservation fee

ELEVATION: 4,800'

RESTRICTIONS:

PETS: On leash only

FIRES: In fire rings only

ALCOHOL: Permitted

VEHICLES: RVs or trailers prohibited;
ATVs prohibited

QUIET HOURS: 10 p.m.–6 a.m.

OTHER: 7-day stay limit; firearms prohibited;
radio prohibited; 8-person limit/site;
loud generators prohibited; 1 vehicle/site;
checkout 1 p.m.

only sites 9–19 are reservable, and these lie right along the creekbed. Site 11 is the exception, since it's actually in the flood plain and can only be used when the creek is expected to behave itself.

Both the north and south entrances from AZ 89A lead down to the self-service pay station and the campground host. If you have a reservation, you may continue to your site. If you're hoping for a first-come, first-served site, come early and check with the host—she may not even have time to remove the CAMPGROUND FULL sign before it's true again. Sites 1–3 are level, but close together in the middle of the campground loop, and sites 6 and 7 are also quite open and close to the camp road. Raised above the campground on a leveled shelf, site 5 is a nice, compact site with its back to the highway. Site 4, at the end of the loop, sits a little apart from its neighbors, but for privacy and spaciousness, take 19. You'll need to be able to parallel park for sites 11–15, but the sites are reasonably spaced and right along the creek. If you have a group, sites 9 and 10, past the host in site 8, share parking and almost have a stretch of the creek to themselves (these are also the most accessible sites). The tight loop road discourages trailers and RVs, and the rule is one vehicle per site. You can take a shower five miles north at the much-larger Cave Spring Campground; just let the staff at the entry station know you're camped at Manzanita, and they'll sell you a token.

AZ 89A snakes up the narrow canyon, making traffic noise unavoidable. It will fade into the background, allowing the burble of the creek to come through clearly, and the campground itself is very quiet. The creek flow depends on rainfall and snowmelt, and on rare occasions has risen over the stone retaining walls and swirled around the picnic tables. The campground is in a stand of ponderosa pines, box elders, Gambel oak, and Arizona ash that, along with the high red cliffs, provide ample shade. South of the campground, past sites 9 and 10, the creek opens up to form a large swimming hole, and a trail up the creek passes the foundations of an old homestead with feral apple trees in the front garden.

Just 0.75 mile north of the campground is Slide Rock State Park, where the smooth, slick rock of the creek bottom has created a natural slide popular with families. Thrill seekers also enjoy jumping from the surrounding boulders into the creek's cool pools. An orchard from the park's former life as a farmstead still bears fruit today, and apple picking is one of the park's seasonal activities.

A little farther north is perpetually busy Call of the Canyon Picnic Site, named after the Zane Grey novel set here, and the trailhead for the West Fork Trail—the most popular trail in the Coconino National Forest. This scenic path crosses the stream several times and is rich in wildlife and beautifully weathered rock. The first 3 miles are very heavily used, but if you enjoy bouldering and the occasional swim, you can escape down 14 miles of rugged canyon beyond the developed trail. If the crowd is too much for you, there are many other spectacular hikes in the Sedona area, so pick up a guide, get out on the red rocks, and go!

You'll need to have a national Interagency Pass or purchase a Red Rock Pass to use any of the national forest land in the Sedona area, including hiking trails, picnic areas, and the many ruins and heritage sites; note that the most popular sites, including Grasshopper Point swimming area, Crescent Moon day-use, and Call of the Canyon/West Fork Trailhead, are special fee areas.

Manzanita Campground

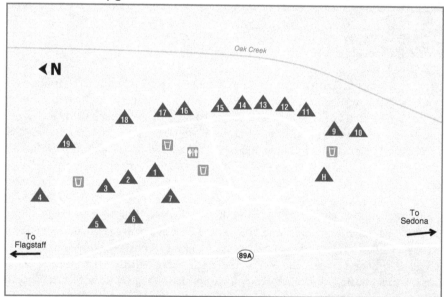

GETTING THERE

From Sedona, take AZ 89A north 6 miles. Turn right into the campground.

GPS COORDINATES N34° 56.145' W111° 44.689'

7

North Rim Campground

Beauty ★★★★★ Privacy ★★★ Spaciousness ★★★★ Quiet ★★★★ Security ★★★★ Cleanliness ★★★★★

Camp at one of several scenic points and have the entire area to yourself.

Arizona abounds with great spots to pitch a tent, but for solitude and sheer, stunning beauty, nothing beats the North Rim of the Grand Canyon. The North Rim is the less known, less popular, harder-to-reach, but just-as-spectacular way to view America's most famous natural wonder. Of the 6 million people who visit the Grand Canyon every year, 90% go to the South Rim and see the canyon from the overlooks. The North Rim sees far fewer visitors and boasts a few places to camp where you might even have the grandeur of the grandest canyon all to yourself.

There's one developed campground inside the park on the North Rim, with 88 tent and RV sites, plus a lodge with cabins for rent. Both the lodge and campground fill up during summer, especially on weekends, and reservations are required (often months in advance). The 12 recently renovated tent spots offer cleared pads across a small ravine from the rest of the campground. Our picks are T4 and T6, away from the main campground and with views of Transept Canyon. There are also several hike-in or bike-in sites designated solely for those without vehicles. If the tent-only area is full, check out the premium sites in the main campground (11, 14–16, or 18). These have smaller, less level tent spots, but better views of the canyon. Transept Trail, the 1.5-mile hike along the rim to North Rim Lodge, begins between sites 15 and 16. Near North Rim Campground you'll find several amenities

Point Sublime lives up to its name for the backcountry adventurer.

KEY INFORMATION

CONTACT: 928-638-7888, nps.gov/grca; reservations: 877-444-6777, recreation.gov

OPEN: Mid-May–mid-October

SITES: 88, plus 3 group sites

EACH SITE HAS: Picnic table, fire ring, tent pads at tent sites

ASSIGNMENT: By reservation

REGISTRATION: Check in at kiosk

AMENITIES: Flush toilets, dump station, hot coin-operated showers, laundry, day-use area, amphitheater, interpretive activities and programs, group area, drinking fountains, firewood, campground host, wheelchair-accessible sites and restrooms, general store

PARKING: At campsites

FEE: $18–$25/night, plus $30/week park-entrance fee

ELEVATION: 8,300'

RESTRICTIONS:

PETS: On leash only; prohibited in wilderness areas, below canyon rim, and on trails except Bridle Trail; pets may not be left unattended, and there are no kennels on the North Rim

FIRES: In fire rings only

ALCOHOL: Permitted

VEHICLES: 2 vehicles/site; 1 vehicle/site in tent sites; vehicle pulling a trailer counts as 2 vehicles

QUIET HOURS: 10 p.m.–6 a.m.

OTHER: Firewood gathering prohibited; 6-person limit/site; 3-tent limit/site; tent sites limited to 1 large or 2 small tents that must be on the tent pad; 7-day stay limit; checkout 10 a.m.

that are blessings to weary hikers, including hot showers, laundry facilities, and a general store with simple groceries and souvenirs. Other services include a bookstore, interpretive programs, gas, a car mechanic, and a dump station.

If you're an experienced winter adventurer, you can hike, snowshoe, or ski in to use the campground on a first-come, first-served basis after the park road has closed for the season. You'll need a backcountry permit, and there are no off-season services.

The self-sufficient camper has more options to escape the crowd. Inside the national park boundary, you must camp in designated campsites or areas only. What most people don't realize is that you can camp at several scenic points with a backcountry permit and have the entire area to yourself, since the park limits the number of permits issued. If you're up for a rough (high-clearance, 4WD) 17-mile drive, Point Sublime offers two sites with eastern views of Confucius Temple, Mencius Temple, Osiris Temple, and Dragon Head—with a bonus of great sunrises. Point Sublime even boasts a composting toilet with open-air charm—so much so, you'll want an umbrella if it's raining.

Primitive at-large camping is available on the Walhalla Plateau, near the Widforss Trail, and in a few other areas, and there's a single designated spot right on the rim down the 2-mile trail to Cape Final. The earlier you plan, the more likely your first choice will be granted. The backcountry office can give you even more options; make reservations online, or if you're more of a last-minute type, drop by the permit office at the North Rim to check for availabilities. Dog owners take note: your pet is not allowed in the park backcountry, even at your campsite. There are no kennel facilities at the North Rim, so it might be better to leave the hounds at home.

There's also terrific dispersed camping in the Kaibab National Forest surrounding the park boundary. Lookout points such as Marbleview, Crazy Jug, and Dog Point require only a drive down a bumpy road to reach overlooks nearly as spectacular as any in the park. Dispersed camping in the national forest is free, and pets are allowed as long as you clean up after them. You must be self-contained since there are no toilets or trash service, but you also have no fees, permits, or reservations to worry about. You can build a campfire in the national forest (with adequate precautions), but not in the national park's backcountry.

Several forested trails along the rim offer great views of the canyon, including the 10-mile Widforss Trail, the 5-mile Uncle Jim Trail, and the 4-mile Cape Final Trail. If you plan to hike into the Grand Canyon on the North Kaibab Trail, be sure to call the backcountry office and plan ahead. You must have a permit to hike overnight, and it is recommended that you not hike more than 10 miles in one day, nor between 10 a.m. and 4 p.m. in the summer. If you plan to hike all the way down the canyon to the Colorado River, you must spend the night at Cottonwood Camp, 7 miles below the rim. The Grand Canyon is an amazing place to visit, so make your visit a safe one. Know the dangers of the canyon—stay a safe distance from the edges, remain on the trails, and drink plenty of water and eat salty snacks while hiking.

One last note: seeing both sides of the canyon in one trip may be difficult—it's only 10 miles across as the crow flies, but it takes at least 5 hours to drive the 220 miles from the South Rim to the North Rim.

North Rim Campground

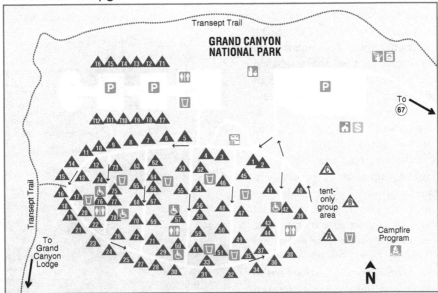

GETTING THERE

From Jacob Lake, take AZ 67 south 30 miles to the park entrance. Continue south 12 miles to the turnoff to the campground. Turn right and head west to the campground entrance.

GPS COORDINATES N36° 12.622' W112° 03.637'

8

⛺ Tuweep/Toroweap Campground

Beauty ★★★★★ Privacy ★★★★ Spaciousness ★★★★ Quiet ★★★★★ Security ★★★★ Cleanliness ★★★★

From here, you can look straight down 3,000 feet into the steepest, narrowest part of the Grand Canyon and see the Colorado River below.

As you leave the highway, signs read PRIMITIVE ROAD, USE AT YOUR OWN RISK, and they mean it. Once you leave Fredonia, you can turn off your useless cell phone and get in the backcountry mindset. The National Park Service recommends you bring extra water, food, gasoline, spare tires, and tools, as vehicles have been stuck for days on the way to Toroweap. The beginning of the drive is sandy, and flocks of sparrows flitter away to avoid your trailing dust plume. As the long washboard road winds on it may be rutted or peppered with rocks and tire-thumping potholes. Take your time (allow 2–3 hours) and enjoy the scenery as it subtly changes from scrub brush to grassy plains to juniper-covered hillsides.

This is nothing like entering Grand Canyon National Park at the South or North Rim. There's no entrance station, and no entrance fee, although you will need to get a backcountry permit before you go. Pick up an area brochure at the tiny Tuweep Ranger Station; the ranger who lives here year-round is often out on patrol, but he'll check in with you once you are settled at the campground. The most difficult stretch of road is the 5.4 miles past the station, where the slickrock is exposed and large, sometimes sharp, rocks are waiting to eat your tires. Once you turn left into the campground, hop out of your vehicle, celebrate your achievement, and check for loose bolts!

The campground rests upon deep shelves carved out of the sandstone of the Toroweap formation by eons of erosion. All of the sites have tremendous views looking out over the pinyon-studded slickrock toward the variegated walls of the canyon. The sites are numbered and well spaced, each with a picnic table. Camping is by permit only, but site assignment is open, so take your pick of empty sites. If you're dependent on stakes to support your tent, be sure to scout carefully—the loose soil is thin over the stone. Much of the land between the sites is being revegetated, so keep to the established trails; a single step can cause years' worth of damage to the delicate black biological crust that forms the top layer of soil.

The first three sites are to the right of the entrance, on slightly higher and more open ground. Site 1 is large with

Follow the endless sky from the campground to the canyon rim.

KEY INFORMATION

CONTACT: 928-638-7888, nps.gov/grca; reservations: 877-444-6777, recreation.gov

OPEN: Year-round when roads are open

SITES: 10

EACH SITE HAS: Picnic table

ASSIGNMENT: First-come, first-served; reservations accepted for group site

REGISTRATION: Advance backcountry permit required; visit nps.gov/grca /planyourvisit/backcountry-permit.htm for more information

AMENITIES: Composting toilets, group site, resident park ranger, and emergency phone located at Tuweep Ranger Station

PARKING: At campsites

FEE: $8/night; $10 online-reservation fee

ELEVATION: 4,600'

RESTRICTIONS:

PETS: On leash only, prohibited on trails, restricted to open roads and campground

FIRES: Prohibited

ALCOHOL: Permitted

VEHICLES: RVs and trailers not recommended; high clearance required; 2 vehicles/site; ATVs, dirt bikes, and vehicles longer than 22 feet prohibited; off-road travel prohibited

QUIET HOURS: 10 p.m.–6 a.m.

OTHER: Pack in/pack out; firearms prohibited; fires and charcoal grills prohibited; 8-person limit/site; collecting, destroying, or disturbing any natural resource prohibited; no drinking water available

plenty of spaces to pitch a tent. Although site 2 is directly across from site 3, you have a terrific view looking toward the canyon. If you're sleeping in your vehicle, level site 3 is a good choice. All three sites are convenient to the first of the two composting toilets in the campground.

Turn left to reach sites 4–10, where the curve of the rim forms a sheltered basin. The camp road traces the edge of the bare stone shelf, so pick your route carefully and watch for grooves in the rock where others have scraped. There's not much of a tent spot at site 4 unless you're willing to pitch your tent in the small wash that also accommodates parking. Climb two or three stone steps to get up to site 5, where a rock wall and pinyon pines provide late-afternoon shade and the world spreads out in front of you. Site 6 is tucked in the bend of the rock walls, with a 90° view across the valley and space for several tents, making this one of the better sites for a small group. Tuck your tent underneath the large rock awning at site 7 and you can easily imagine life as a cliff dweller, but be sure to look for telltale signs of flowing water before choosing your spot if you're here during a rainy season.

Continue around the rim to site 8, which sits underneath a huge mushrooming boulder with lots of afternoon shade. Nearby, site 9 is also tucked underneath projecting rock with a couple of nicely sheltered tent spots. There's a touch of history in this sheltered spot— stacked rocks in natural openings between the boulders create walls with windows, and peeling plaster attests to the effort of the bygone cowboy, prospector, or hermit who built a tiny shelter here. Out on the flat rock shelf, two picnic tables and a fire ring constitute group site 10. There is plenty of room here to pitch several tents, but be aware of foot traffic as other campers head for the Tuckup Trail through your site (see next page).

Once you have chosen your site, hike the 1.6-mile round-trip Saddle Horse Loop Trail or drive to the spectacular Toroweap Overlook. From here, you can look straight down 3,000 feet into the steepest, narrowest part of the Grand Canyon and see the Colorado River below. Even from this height you can hear the roar of Lava Falls, the most dangerous rapid on the river. Be sure to watch your step and keep a close eye on children; there are no barriers here.

Old maps show two more campsites at the overlook, but these have since been converted to a day-use-only picnic area. For a choose-your-own-length hike with a few more challenges, explore the Tuckup Trail. This route continues for almost 60 miles, but the first 3 are on a fairly level old roadbed, and there's is a great view of the river that makes a nice turnaround point. If you choose to go farther, make sure you've got a good topo, some wayfinding skills, and read the National Park Service route description and cautions.

If you were unable to secure a backcountry permit, backtrack outside the park boundary to Grand Canyon–Parashant National Monument for dispersed camping. You'll discover some particularly nice spots among the junipers along the Mount Trumbull Road. The road continues west and climbs into a ponderosa forest near the 6,500-foot peak of Mount Trumbull, an extinct volcano. In this rarely visited area, the 5-mile hike to the peak abounds with wildlife. This scenic drive eventually winds up in St. George, Utah. Three hours west of Toroweap at the Whitmore Overlook, you can hike all the way down to the Colorado River along the moderately difficult 4-mile Whitmore Trail; as always, be sure you have the proper permits and are thoroughly prepared for a canyon trek.

Tuweep/Toroweap Campground

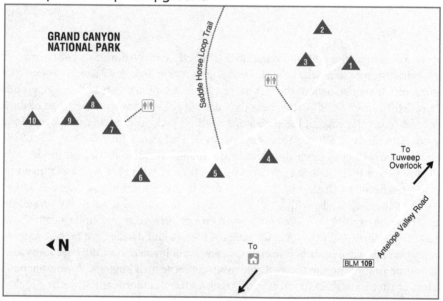

GETTING THERE

From Fredonia, take AZ 389 west 7 miles to Antelope Valley Road (BLM Road 109). Turn left and continue south 61 miles to campground.

GPS COORDINATES N36° 13.367' W113° 03.690'

9

The View Campground

Beauty ★★★★★ Privacy ★ Spaciousness ★ Quiet ★★★★ Security ★★★★ Cleanliness ★★★★

You can easily pretend that nothing but the little line of tents and the ancient landscape exist.

Mention Monument Valley and most people can immediately picture two vast upraised hands of sandstone, glowing red in the light of sunset. These iconic monoliths set the stage for dozens of films, becoming a quintessential symbol of the American West. Director John Ford started the trend with *Stagecoach* in 1939 and was apparently so fond of the location that he shot *The Searchers* here despite the fact that the story was set in Texas. The valley has since appeared in everything from *2001: A Space Odyssey* to *The Lego Movie.*

Called *Tse'Bii'Ndzisgaii,* or "Valley of Rocks," by the Diné, these siltstone-capped towers are what remains of ancient sediments originally washed down from the Rockies after centuries of erosion have swept the surrounding shale away. Iron oxide in the stone gives the majestic East and West Mittens and other unique formations their characteristic red color. This land is home to many Diné families, and Monument Valley Navajo Tribal Park, with its newly renovated hotel, cabins, and campground, offers the only gateway for visitors to experience this landscape more intimately.

The Mittens greet you when you wake up at The View.

KEY INFORMATION

CONTACT: 435-727-5802,
monumentvalleyview.com/campground

OPEN: Mid-March–mid-November

SITES: 30

EACH SITE HAS: Space to pitch a tent—
no picnic tables or fire rings

ASSIGNMENT: First-come, first-served or
by reservation

REGISTRATION: At office or front desk

AMENITIES: Flush toilets, showers,
visitor center, gift shop, free Wi-Fi

PARKING: In designated lot

FEE: $19.95/night plus tax (credit card only);
$20 Monument Valley entry fee (cash only)

ELEVATION: 5,564'

RESTRICTIONS:

PETS: Prohibited

FIRES: Prohibited

ALCOHOL: Prohibited

VEHICLES: No length limit

QUIET HOURS: 10 p.m.–6 a.m.

OTHER: No stay limit; no group limit if
tents fit; group campsite available for
a minimum of 30 people

The View Campground consists of an RV park and 30 walk-in tent spots that are little more than a stake in the sand. You won't find a picnic table or fire ring (campfires are prohibited), and there's not much elbow room between the vaguely defined sites, but the campground is full most nights. Your neighbors are unlikely to be partiers who plan on staying up all night (alcohol is also prohibited in the Navajo Nation); what you will find is people who are excited by the prospect of waking at sunrise to catch that perfect photo of the sun rising behind West Mitten, possibly taken from their sleeping bag. Nothing impairs the view from the View over Monument Valley. While the campground may be bare bones, the rest of the developed park is above the ridge, and you can easily pretend that nothing but the little line of tents and the ancient landscape exist.

When you arrive at the View, check in at the office or at the hotel after hours. This isn't a campground to roll into after dark, however, since you'll need a bit of creative discernment to find the site boundaries. With map in hand, you can walk through the sites and choose your favorite view. We recommend sites 29 and 30 for the most privacy, although be prepared to be a mere 15–30 feet from your neighbor with only rabbitbrush and blackbrush for screening. The ground is fine red sand, which can make for very comfortable sleeping, but also stays with you and your gear as an unavoidable souvenir.

From the east side of the campground, you can take the Wildcat Trail hike around West Mitten. This scenic 3.8-mile loop hike circumnavigates the butte with breathtaking views and wonderful photo opportunities. For a bird's-eye view of the landscape, hike the moderately difficult 0.7-mile Mesa Rim Trail. To make a loop hike, take the 2.1-mile Lee Cly Trail, named after a Diné man who was born at Monument Valley in the early 1950s and spent his entire career as a tribal park employee.

Be sure to take the scenic drive around the valley and learn the names creatively applied to formations such as the Three Sisters and Elephant Butte. A high-clearance vehicle is required, and the road may be impassible during monsoon season; the park may close during truly inclement weather. If you don't have a capable vehicle, don't worry. You can hire a Navajo guide to take you around and even to some sites only open to tour guides, such as Ear of the Wind and Sleeping Dragon. For a more authentic Western experience, you can take the tour on horseback or, if your posterior isn't up for it, simply have your photo taken in the saddle at John Ford Point.

During the summer be sure to stop at the Haskenneini Restaurant in the visitor center for a Navajo meal with an extraordinary view. The museum in the visitor center showcases Navajo culture as well as the geology of the area. There's a gift shop, and numerous Navajo vendors sell arts, crafts, and souvenirs throughout the park.

There are many other unique destinations on the Navajo Nation to visit, so with a bit of planning you can stand in four states at once at the Four Corners Monument, explore the picturesque slot canyons of Antelope Canyon, see the White House ruins at Canyon de Chelly National Monument, meet the animals native to the area at the Navajo Nation Botanical and Zoological Park, and hike to the Keet Seel ruins (for more information about Keet Seel and other archaeological sites, see profile 1, Canyon View Campground, page 15). A permit is required for any hiking or camping on the Navajo Nation, so be sure to check with tribal authorities as you plan. Note that the Navajo Nation follows daylight savings time, whereas the rest of Arizona does not.

The View Campground

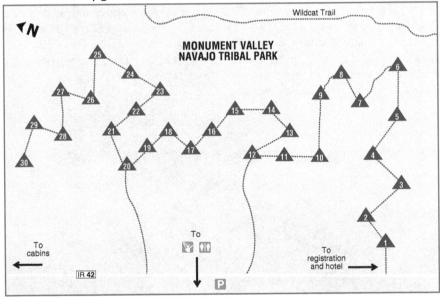

GETTING THERE

From Kayenta, take US 163 north 23 miles past the Arizona–Utah border to Monument Valley Road. Turn right and drive southeast 3 miles back across the Arizona border on Indian Route 42 to the park entrance.

GPS COORDINATES N36° 59.128' W110° 07.170'

10

White Horse Lake Campground

Beauty ★★★ Privacy ★★★ Spaciousness ★★★★★ Quiet ★★★ Security ★★★★ Cleanliness ★★★★★

Cool temperatures and tall pine forests make this area a favorite getaway.

Situated on old Route 66, the city of Williams survived the arrival of the interstate and thrives on tourism in the Western theme, with steakhouses galore and gunfights staged on Main Street every summer evening. Cowboys, both live and animatronic, can be found singin', gun-slingin', and even stilt-walkin' through the crowds passing by the antiques stores, gift shops, restaurants, and bevy of saloons. If cowboys prove too tame for you, grizzled mountain men still follow the tradition of the town's namesake; pioneer and trapper William Sherley Williams, affectionately called "Old Bill," traveled through the area in the early 1800s. The Bill Williams Mountain Men celebrate the pioneer spirit of Old Bill during the annual Rendezvous Ride, a 200-mile charity horseback ride from Williams to Phoenix, with riders dressed in fur, buckskins, and an impressive array of beards.

What first brought mountain men and ranchers and then lumbermen and railways to Williams were the trees. The area shares Flagstaff's cool temperatures and tall pine forests, making it a haven for wildlife and a rich resource for early settlers. Seven lakes and reservoirs dot this area of the Kaibab National Forest, along with several campgrounds. You can also enjoy dispersed camping in the national forest, as long as you camp at least 0.25 mile from any water source. Some areas see very heavy use, and in the summer you'll find RVs and ATVs scattered throughout the woods.

Sycamore Canyon is one of Arizona's many Technicolor wonders.

KEY INFORMATION

CONTACT: 928-635-5600, tinyurl.com /whitehorselake; reservations: 877-444-6777, recreation.gov

OPEN: Full services May 1–October 1, depending on weather and roads

SITES: 89 (8 walk-in tent sites)

EACH SITE HAS: Picnic table, fire ring; some sites have an upright grill

ASSIGNMENT: First-come, first-served; reservations available online for 44 single sites and group site

REGISTRATION: Self-register on-site or online

AMENITIES: Composting toilets, pit toilets, water spigots, recycling, picnic areas, day-use ramadas, boat launch, dump station, firewood, nature trail, wheelchair-accessible sites, food vendor

PARKING: At campsites

FEE: $24/night single, $40/night double, $12/additional vehicle; $10 online-reservation fee

ELEVATION: 7,000'

RESTRICTIONS:

PETS: On leash only

FIRES: In fire rings

ALCOHOL: Permitted

VEHICLES: 38-foot limit

QUIET HOURS: 10 p.m.–6 a.m.

OTHER: Swimming prohibited; small electric boat motors only; 14-day stay limit

Our favorite campground is White Horse Lake, about half an hour from downtown Williams; close enough to partake in the festivities, yet far enough away to enjoy a peaceful evening by the campfire. Pavement gives way to good graded all-weather roads about 10 miles from the campground, but be on the lookout for unusual slowdowns—you'll never believe how many different noises sheep can make until your car is trapped in a flock of hundreds.

White Horse is easily accessible to RVs, but lack of hookups means there's usually a balance of tin cans and tent campers. The campground itself is paved to keep the dust down, and every site has a generous leveled tent pad plus picnic table and fire ring. There are also fully accessible sites with concrete bibs, paved paths, and upright grills in every loop (22 sites in all), making this the most wheelchair-friendly campground we've seen. This is ponderosa forest, so there's no undergrowth, but most sites have a fair amount of elbow room, and the mighty pines provide substantial shade.

As you enter the campground, loops A and B will be to your right. Most sites here have at least a sliver of lake view, and we particularly recommend sites A15, A19, A21, B35 and B36, where you can set up your chair with your back to your neighbors and admire the water. There's a day-use area by the lake between the two loops that hosts a snack wagon during the season.

Take a left at the intersection near the campground entrance, and your next stop is loop C, where you'll find eight walk-in tent sites on a shallow point. We especially like sites C53, farthest out on the point, and C58. C51 looks back toward a small inlet and is nicely separated from the other sites. C56 and C57 are quite close together and would be best for a larger party. The accessible sites in this loop are C52 and C54, with paved paths from two designated handicapped-parking spaces. Past loop C you'll find the boat ramp and loop D—the best sites here are D64 (fully accessible), D65, and D66. Most of the sites in loop E do not have a lake view and will probably see less use, so look here if the campground is near capacity.

The 35-acre lake is open to small human- or electric-powered boats, but swimming is not allowed. The water sport of choice here is fishing, for rainbow and brown trout and channel catfish. You can stroll around the lakeshore from one end of the campground to the other on White Horse Lake Trail 33, starting near the group site in loop F. This intersects with the Canyon Overlook Trail 70, a 2.5-mile hike to a vista of one of Arizona's undeveloped gems, Sycamore Canyon. This stunning wilderness canyon shares the famous red rock of Sedona but is far less accessible and less well known. Contact the U.S. Forest Service to find out more about the hiking trails along the rim and in the canyon itself.

To the north, of course, there's another small attraction; Williams has actually trademarked the motto "Gateway to the Grand Canyon." The Atchison, Topeka and Santa Fe Railroad Company began carrying passengers from here to the Grand Canyon in 1901. In 1989, retired entrepreneurs Max and Thelma Biegert brought the deserted line back to life, and today the Grand Canyon Railway is one of the main tourist attractions in Williams. The 2-hour-and-15-minute ride takes passengers from downtown Williams directly to Grand Canyon Village. Choose your style, from Pullman coach to luxurious parlor, or even ride high in a glass-domed observation car. Singing cowboys, fully stocked bars, and (of course) a train robbery highlight the trip.

White Horse Lake Campground

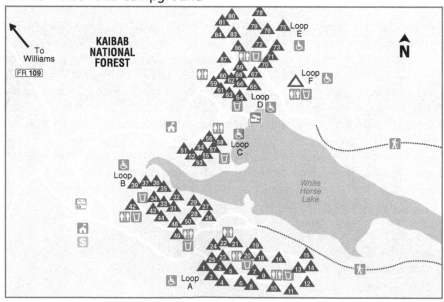

GETTING THERE

From Williams, take Fourth Street (Forest Road 173–Perkinsville Road) south 9 miles to FR 110. Turn left and continue east 7 miles to FR 109. Turn left and drive northeast 3 miles to the campground.

GPS COORDINATES N35° 07.083' W112° 01.281'

11

Wild Cow Springs Recreation Site Campground

Beauty ★★★★ Privacy ★★★ Spaciousness ★★★ Quiet ★★★ Security ★★★ Cleanliness ★★★★

The mountains offer a nice respite during the hot summer months and a great escape year-round.

Getting to Wild Cow Springs Recreation Site is part of the fun. The drive takes you up into the Hualapai Mountains, steadily climbing 3,000 feet above the Kingman Valley below. The mountains, covered in Gambel oak, ponderosa pines, and craggy granite rock offer a nice respite during the hot summer months and a great escape year-round. The oaks blaze yellow in the fall; in winter, snow often blankets the mountains and provides smooth hills to sled. Spring sprinkles the forest floor with wildflowers.

Past the small community of Pine Lake, the paved road becomes dirt, very narrow, and rough, so a high-clearance vehicle with good tires is highly recommended; RVs and all but the smallest trailers definitely are not. The road climbs steadily with sheer drop-offs. You may be tempted to enjoy the splendid view of distant mountains spreading out below you, but keep your eyes on the road; no guardrail prevents that look from becoming a leap! After climbing over a ridge, you switchback down the other side of the mountain (which affords more great views) before coming to the Wild Cow Springs Recreation Site. You'll find the 18 campsites along a bumpy dirt up-and-back road. Stop at the pay station to pick up a self-pay envelope, and check out the tiny, picturesque cabin that is actually the first set of vault toilets.

A touch of welcome rain brushes a corner of the Hualapai Mountains.

KEY INFORMATION

CONTACT: 928-718-3700, blm.gov/visit/wild-cow-springs-campground

OPEN: Year-round when roads are open

SITES: 18

EACH SITE HAS: Picnic table, fire ring

ASSIGNMENT: First-come, first-served; no reservations

REGISTRATION: Self-register on-site

AMENITIES: Vault toilets, group sites, wheelchair-accessible sites

PARKING: At campsites

FEE: $8/night standard site, $20/night for group site

ELEVATION: 6,200'

RESTRICTIONS:

PETS: On leash only

FIRES: In fire rings only

ALCOHOL: Permitted

VEHICLES: 20-foot length limit; high clearance recommended; RVs and trailers not recommended

QUIET HOURS: 10 p.m.–6 a.m.

OTHER: 14-day stay limit; discharging of firearms prohibited; no drinking water available

Site 1, a small site located just off the road next to the group area, is immediately on your left. The unnumbered group area is available first-come, first-served, costs $20 instead of $8, and offers five picnic tables, a large upright grill, and a fire ring. Site 2 is large, with a cleared, slightly raised tenting spot next to the road but sheltered by lots of underbrush. The site, which has a lot of room between the picnic table and fire ring, is within easy walking distance of the toilet chalet. The Civilian Conservation Corps (CCC) built the campground in the 1930s, and although erosion has taken its toll in some areas, most of the sites are still nicely leveled and bordered by rock walls.

In the parking tab next to site 2, posts point out the hiking trail, lined by stones, that travels between the sites. Take this trail to get to walk-in sites 3–6, in the oaks across the canyon. You must cross the creekbed in order to get to these sites, which could be tricky after dark or after heavy rainfall or snowmelt. When the creek is flowing in the small but steep ravine, a miniature waterfall cascades down the rocks near site 6. Site 7 is a wheelchair-accessible site right off the road with a paved path to nearby toilets. Site 8 requires a short walk-in and is surrounded by boulders. Your picnic table here is precariously close to the edge of the ravine, but the site is nicely secluded and screened by oak trees. Sites 9–12 are on the opposite side of the road, and all except 11 require a short uphill hike on paths hidden behind brush and oak. Sites 13–17 sit closer together with their backs to the ravine. These sites tend to be more popular with pop-up trailers or truck campers since the parking tabs are wider and flatter.

If you don't have a high-clearance vehicle or you'd like to stay somewhere more developed, stop at Hualapai Mountain Park instead of heading down past Pine Lake. This Mohave County park offers 70 campsites among ponderosa pines and large granite boulders, rustic rental cabins, or outfitter tents for rent. Most folks with RVs will stay here at the small RV park instead of trying to make it down the road to Wild Cow Springs. Also near Pine Lake is the Hualapai Mountain Resort, which offers lodging and a great place to watch the elk as you dine.

From the Hualapai Mountain Park, a $7 day-use fee allows you to hike, bike, or horseback ride 10 miles of trails in a trail system originally built by the CCC. Paths lead up to

Aspen Peak (7,950'), Hayden Peak (8,250'), and Hualapai Peak (8,250'). Also nearby is the Wabayuma Peak Wilderness, with a trail leading to its 7,601-foot summit. High clearance and four-wheel drive is recommended to access the wilderness. There are also several ATV trails around Wild Cow Springs and the Pine Flat community.

If you have time, take a side trip to the historic mining town of Oatman, just 28 miles southwest of Kingman on Historic Route 66, a National Scenic Byway. Oatman, today a thriving tourist town with restaurants and gift shops, is best known for its "wild" burros—descendants of the early miners' pack animals.

Wild Cow Springs Recreation Site Campground

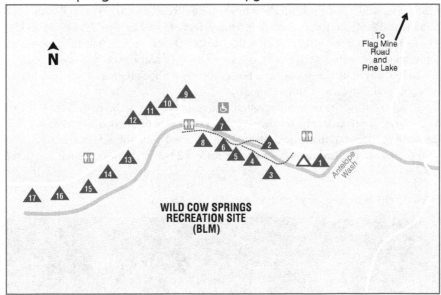

GETTING THERE

From Kingman, take Hualapai Mountain Road southeast 14 miles to the small community of Pine Lake. Turn right at Flag Mine Road and drive 4 miles to Wild Cow Springs Recreation Site.

GPS COORDINATES N35° 03.875' W113° 52.155'

12

Windy Point Recreation Site Campground

Beauty ★★★★ Privacy ★★★★ Spaciousness ★★★★ Quiet ★★★★ Security ★★★ Cleanliness ★★★

Each site has a great view of the valley below and very little view of its neighbors.

Most people who make the drive from Kingman to Las Vegas don't pay much attention to the rugged, forlorn-looking hills to the east. The Cerbat Mountains have their secrets, however, including wild horses, several ghost towns (one alive and well), and two Bureau of Land Management (BLM) campgrounds. To get there, leave US 93 at Big Wash Road and begin the climb up into the mountains. This is the Mojave Desert, whose barren expanses make the Sonoran Desert with its trademark saguaros seem verdant by comparison. It seems surprising to find anything green out here, but as you switchback higher up the winding road, the air cools and pinyon and juniper appear.

Tiny Packsaddle is the first campground you come to, where the road crosses the spine of the Cerbats. There are four sites here—two on each side of the road—tucked among the junipers and available at no charge. Follow the rock-lined path uphill to reach the two small sites on the right. The fire rings have been reinforced by extra rocks, which suggested to

Artist Roy Purcell's new-age visions glow from the rocks near Chloride.

KEY INFORMATION

CONTACT: 928-718-3700, blm.gov/visit
/windy-point

OPEN: Year-round

SITES: 7

EACH SITE HAS: Picnic table, fire ring

ASSIGNMENT: First-come, first-served;
no reservations

REGISTRATION: Self-register on-site

AMENITIES: Vault toilets

PARKING: At campsites

FEE: $8/night

ELEVATION: 6,200'

RESTRICTIONS:

PETS: On leash only

FIRES: In fire rings only

ALCOHOL: Permitted

VEHICLES: Travel trailers not recommended

QUIET HOURS: 10 p.m.–6 a.m.

OTHER: 14-day stay limit; discharging of firearms prohibited; no drinking water available

us chilly nights for previous campers. Large pinyon pines shade parts of site 1. Sites 3 and 4, across the road, are a bit larger and the ground is more level. Site 3 has a generous tent area hidden among the trees and an upright grill. Packsaddle might offer a bit more shelter when gales roar over the ridge, but we recommend that you sign in at the BLM logbook and continue the additional 1.5 miles to Windy Point.

The road takes you along the ridgeline and out to a rocky spur, where seven sites over-look the old mining town of Chloride. The campground is arranged in a loop with all of the sites radiating out. Ample room exists between the sites, and each one has a great view of the valley below and very little view of its neighbors. The pinyon and juniper are joined here by manzanita and scrub live oak. Windy Point is aptly named, so be sure to bring your windbreaker and secure your tent well.

Site 1, nestled against a mound of boulders, sees a bit of the road but none of the rest of the campground. It offers a large, sandy tent area and a pinyon-shaded picnic table. Site 2 is compact, but doesn't feel it, with pinyons providing a touch of shade. One of the tent-able areas at site 3 sits right on the edge of a terrific view; with two tables and several tent spots, this would be a good site for a larger family. Site 4 also features some sheltering boul-ders—no shade, but plenty of privacy. A short trail from site 5 leads out to a rocky outcrop. The picnic table and fire pit at site 6 are below the level of the parking tab, between a large pinyon and a juniper, with a large, flat tent area open to the afternoon sun and a view of Cherum Peak. Site 7 is similar, a bit roomier but with less shade. The tent pad faces west, with views stretching for miles.

Spend the afternoon hiking the 3-mile Cherum Peak Trail up 1,000 feet through pin-yons and chaparral to the Cerbats' second-highest point. From here you can see four states: Utah, Nevada, California, and Arizona. The trail was forged and has been maintained by volunteers as well as by the Arizona Conservation Corps, a career-building program for young adults. While hiking to the 6,983-foot summit, keep an eye out for rattlesnakes and the mustangs that roam the Cerbat Mountains. The hardy wild horses are believed to be descendants of mounts that escaped or were stolen from Spanish explorers. The BLM cur-rently manages the herd very lightly, as the mountain lions that also thrive in this area do a good job of keeping the population in balance. Peregrine falcons nest in the cliffs and spires of the Cerbat Pinnacles, an impressive geologic formation in the Mount Tipton Wilderness that crowns the Cerbats north of Big Wash Road. There are no maintained trails in the wilderness, so you'll need topo maps and route-finding skills to hike there; the BLM will happily provide more information.

The thriving ghost town of Chloride is in the foothills of the Cerbats. Experienced drivers with high-clearance four-wheel drive can dare the rocky two-track road from Windy Point through the remains of several mines to get to the town, or for an easier drive you can head back to the highway. Named after silver chloride that was mined in the Cerbat Mountains, Chloride was home to nearly 2,000 people at the turn of the 20th century. Today, the population is closer to 300, but many of the old buildings still stand and the eclectic mix of inhabitants keeps the atmosphere lively. You can shop for art or antiques, sit down to a meal at Yesterday's restaurant in the old Butterfield stage stop, see the oldest still-operating post office in Arizona, catch an all-female gunfight show by the Wild Roses, and view unique new-age rock murals painted by artist Roy Purcell.

Windy Point Recreation Site Campground

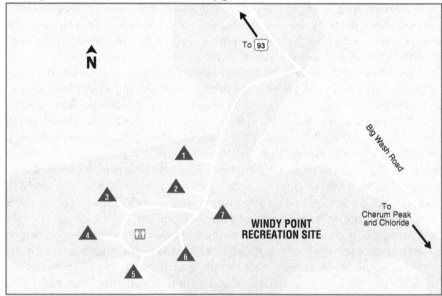

GETTING THERE

From Kingman, take US 93 northwest 18 miles to Big Wash Road. Turn right and drive 10 miles to the campground entrance. Turn right into the campground.

GPS COORDINATES N35° 26.238' W114° 09.510'

CENTRAL ARIZONA

Granite Mountain admires its reflection near Yavapai Campground (campground 25, page 88).

13

Burnt Corral Recreation Site Campground

Beauty ★★★★ Privacy ★★★ Spaciousness ★★ Quiet ★★ Security ★★★ Cleanliness ★★★

Burnt Corral offers plenty of shade and an unobstructed vista of the lake.

Apache Lake, formed by Horse Mesa Dam, is the second-largest of the four reservoirs on the Salt River northeast of Phoenix. All of the lakes in the chain are more or less within easy reach of the Phoenix metropolitan area. To get to them, you twist and wind your way along the Apache Trail National Scenic Byway, past Lost Dutchman State Park and along Canyon Lake. If you've got the munchies, stop at the restaurant and general store at the ghost town of Tortilla Flat, just past Canyon Lake. The Apache Trail turns to dirt shortly after this but is well maintained and poses no trouble for a carefully driven sedan. You might want to park at the Fish Creek bridge and hike along the canyon bottom, scrambling your own way around the boulders. After a wet season, you'll see numerous waterfalls and pools, and may even find yourself taking a compulsory swim or two. During fall or early winter, the sycamores and cottonwoods that line the creek burst into color. This area is prone to flash floods, so be sure to check the weather forecast before exploring the canyon.

Toward the eastern end of 17-mile Apache Lake, you will come to Burnt Corral Recreation Site. The campground is laid out in a long, one-way loop with bisecting roads and a couple of extra loops at the beginning and end. A host lives here all year. Sites are designated

A variety of fish hide beneath Apache Lake's rippled surface.

KEY INFORMATION

CONTACT: 602-225-5395, tinyurl.com
/burntcorral

OPEN: Year-round

SITES: 79

EACH SITE HAS: Picnic table, fire ring; some
have an upright grill; some have a ramada

ASSIGNMENT: First-come, first-served;
no reservations

REGISTRATION: Self-register on-site

AMENITIES: Vault toilets, water spigots,
boat ramp, beach, picnic area, campground hosts, life jacket loaner station

PARKING: At campsites

FEE: $12/night single, $24/night double

ELEVATION: 1,900'

RESTRICTIONS:

PETS: On leash only

FIRES: In fire rings only

ALCOHOL: Permitted

VEHICLES: 22-foot length limit;
2 vehicles/site

QUIET HOURS: 10 p.m.–6 a.m.

OTHER: 14-day stay limit; shooting of
firearms prohibited; 10-person limit/site;
generators may be run 6 a.m.–10 p.m.
September–May, 24 hours/day
June–August

as single, double, triple, or quadruple, with corresponding limits on occupancy, but you pay the same price no matter the size of the site. Take a right up toward sites 4–13 if you'd like to be away from the crowds yet overlook the lake; expect these sites to be warmer, in summer or winter, than those along the shore. Creosote, jojoba, paloverde, and ocotillo surround and screen these sites. Continuing down the loop, desert vegetation gives way to a canopy of mesquite trees. The sites that don't have mesquites to shade them have thoughtfully been built with ramadas. Beware of some of the inner sites such as 15 and 25—they appear to be private, but once you set up camp you'll realize that you're closer to the neighbors than you thought.

As you come around the loop, you'll see that all of the sites on the southern edge sit directly on the water. If possible, try to snag site 36, at the end of a point with a 180° view of the lake. Along the rocky shoreline, either mesquites or ramadas shade compact sites 37, 40, and 42. Site 44 is also on the shore, but note that it sits across from group site 31, which can accommodate several large groups. Sites 52 and 53 are across the road from the swimming beach, with plenty of shade and an unobstructed view of the lake. Screening is minimal along the lakeshore, but sites 58, 60, and 62 have a lot of space and are shaded by mature mesquites. If the campground is full or if you want a more private experience, pitch your tent in the Lower Burnt Corral Dispersed Area, southeast of the campground at the mouth of a sandy wash. These more primitive sites also have mesquite shade, picnic tables, fire rings, and nearby vault toilets.

You'll enjoy the experience more if you adjust your expectations to include plenty of other people. These lakes are always busy, especially during the summer months when Phoenicians try to escape the heat-trapping concrete city. The campground is surrounded by national forest land, including the Four Peaks Wilderness, Three Bar Wildlife Area, and the Superstition Wilderness. Hunters camp here during the fall and winter seasons, and the area attracts serious fishermen with crappie, catfish, smallmouth bass, largemouth bass, carp, walleye, and rainbow trout. The boat ramp near the day-use picnic area comes complete with a life jacket loaner station. A trail leaves the campground at the northern end and heads toward a great shoreline fishing spot and to dispersed shoreline camping at Upper Burnt Corral.

When planning your visit, check srpwater.com/dwr for information on current lake levels, which can vary quite a bit. Nearby Apache Lake Marina and Resort offers boat rentals, a motel, a restaurant, and a small grocery store. Heading north, you can get close to history in the Salado cliff dwellings of Tonto National Monument (see the next profile, Cholla Campground, for more details).

Burnt Corral Recreation Site Campground

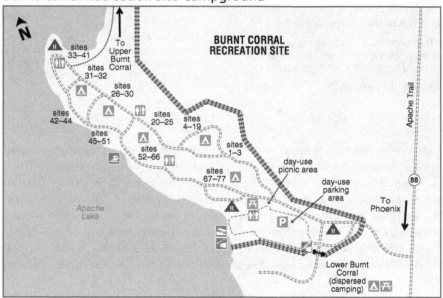

GETTING THERE

From Phoenix, take AZ 88 (the Apache Trail) north 38 miles to Forest Road 183. Turn left to reach the campground entrance.

GPS COORDINATES N33° 37.487' W111° 12.070'

14

Cholla Campground

Beauty ★★★★ Privacy ★★★★ Spaciousness ★★★ Quiet ★★ Security ★★★★ Cleanliness ★★★★

If you're willing to haul your gear, you have a good chance of getting prime camping real estate all to yourself.

Modern Phoenicians know the Salt River Project (SRP) as the folks who send the electric bill every month, but settlers in the early 1900s didn't worry about such newfangled stuff. They started the SRP, using their land as collateral for a government loan, to build a much-needed water delivery system for their homes and crops. The loan was the first one granted under the auspices of the new National Reclamation Act in 1903, and both the dam and lake it created were named in honor of the US president who helped make it possible, Theodore Roosevelt. Within a short time, turbines were installed and additional dams were built along the Salt River, including Horse Mesa Dam (which created Apache Lake), Mormon Flat Dam (Canyon Lake), and Stuart Mountain Dam (Saguaro Lake). Almost as a side effect, the area became a mecca for boaters and fishermen.

This is still a desert, however, and the U.S. Forest Service took that into account when naming Roosevelt Lake's nicest campground (also the largest all-solar-powered campground in the United States). All six loops are named after different types of cholla (pronounced *choy-ah*), a type of cactus with very sharp, barbed spines. The most notorious varieties are

The rugged Sierra Ancha Mountains are sandwiched between blue sky and blue water.

KEY INFORMATION

CONTACT: 602-225-5395, tinyurl.com
/chollacampground

OPEN: Year-round

SITES: 206 (18 walk-in tent sites)

EACH SITE HAS: Picnic table, fire
ring, ramada

ASSIGNMENT: First-come, first-served;
no reservations

REGISTRATION: Self-register on-site

AMENITIES: Vault toilets, flush toilets,
hot showers, water spigots, boat ramp,
drinking fountains, campground host,
recycling, fish-cleaning stations, fishing
docks, playground

PARKING: At campsites, group parking for
walk-in sites

FEE: $20/night single, $40/night double

ELEVATION: 2,200'

RESTRICTIONS:

PETS: On leash only

FIRES: In fire rings only

ALCOHOL: Permitted

VEHICLES: 32-foot length limit; 2 vehicles/
1 watercraft/single site; 4 vehicles/2 water-
craft/double site

QUIET HOURS: 10 p.m.–6 a.m.

OTHER: 14-day stay limit April–September;
6-month stay limit October–March; shooting of firearms prohibited; 10-person limit/
single site; 20-person limit/double site;
generators allowed to run 24 hours June
1–September 30

the teddy bear, which looks so soft that you might be tempted to pet one (don't try it!) and the jumping cholla, which they *say* doesn't actually jump, but is devilishly clever at using your skin, clothing, or dog as transportation for propagation. Once it catches on, it's extremely reluctant to let go.

Like almost all of Arizona's lake campgrounds, Cholla was built to be RV friendly. You could easily imagine making a home here, with hot showers, a playground for the kids, and a gorgeous view, and indeed some people now do just that. Cholla Campground offers long-term stays (up to six months) between October 1 and March 31, which especially appeal to snowbirds, our seasonal visitors from the snowy states. Don't despair at the sight of all the satellite dishes. You'll find 18 walk-in, tent-only sites to get away from the generators, although you can expect to hear boat engines throughout the day.

Stop at the Cane Cholla loop first. The host here says that the tent-only sites rarely get used, so if you are willing to haul your gear 50–400 feet from your car, you may well claim prime real estate all to yourself. Of the five sites at Cane Cholla, site 18 is the best. As the farthest site on the end of the point, it boasts terrific views up and across the lake. Jojoba, paloverde, desert broom, and Mormon tea screen the loop's sites well. Park in front of the restrooms for all five sites.

To get to the second tenting area, with 13 sites and six parking areas, continue to the last loop, Christmas Cholla. Sites 1 and 2 are adjacent, with large tent areas, and would suit a large group. The sites share great views of the Sierra Anchas and of Four Peaks. Site 3 claims the same views but is more secluded. Sites 4 and 5 sit closest to the parking area and are within sight of each other. Sites 6 and 7 are a bit more private and great lake views will reward you. You can hike down to a fishing spot from the parking near site 7. Sites 8 and 9 are a good 100 feet away from the parking area and feel secluded. They look down toward Bermuda Flat, a winter migration area for hundreds of Canada geese. Tall mesquite shrubs somewhat obscure the lake view at sites 11–13, but you can still enjoy the surrounding mountains. A path runs along the outside of all the loops, connecting them and leading out to scenic overlooks. Water attracts wildlife, including wild burros, geese, ducks, eagles, bighorn sheep, mule, deer, javelina, and quail. Fishermen can cast for largemouth and small-mouth bass, crappie, sunfish, catfish, and carp. Just east of the dam, Roosevelt Lake Marina offers bait and tackle, boat rentals, and a floating hotel.

Temperatures here can easily reach a sweltering 120°F in the summer, but winter days are very pleasant. Each loop has its own host, each of whom resides in the campground from November 1 to April 1. Loops close when the campground reaches capacity, with the busiest times being holiday weekends (except Christmas).

While in the area, be sure to visit Tonto National Monument and see the 700-year-old cliff dwellings of the Salado people. From the visitor center, you can climb 350 feet on the 1-mile round-trip hike to the Lower Cliff Dwelling. You must make reservations for the ranger-led tours of the Upper Cliff Dwelling, reached by climbing 600 feet in 1.5 miles. Tours are only offered on weekends November–April, and pets are not allowed on the trails.

Cholla Campground

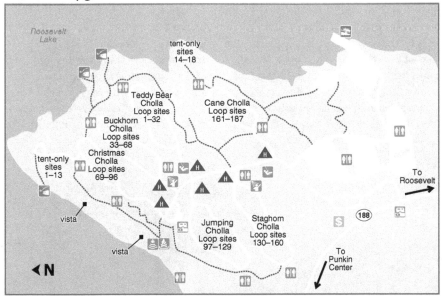

GETTING THERE

From Phoenix, take AZ 87 north 60 miles to AZ 188. Turn right and drive south 28 miles to the campground.

GPS COORDINATES N33° 43.397' W111° 12.307'

15

⛺ Desert Tortoise Campground

Beauty ★★★★ Privacy ★★ Spaciousness ★★★ Quiet ★ Security ★★★★ Cleanliness ★★★★

Portage down to the shore and begin exploring the lake right from your campsite.

Arizonans like to boast that we have more boats per capita than any other state. Whether this is true or not, you'll believe it on a hot day at Lake Pleasant. If you can't escape the valley entirely when it's 100°F in the shade, the next best thing is to find the nearest large body of water. For a lot of metropolitan Phoenix, this is it. In spring and fall, and even at the height of summer, you can expect the lake to be covered in boats and the shoreline dotted with people.

Two campgrounds accommodate the many visitors to Lake Pleasant: Desert Tortoise and Roadrunner. Roadrunner's 72 developed sites sit atop the hill near the visitor center, overlooking the lake. These sites provide electricity and water and, unsurprisingly, are popular with RVs. In the three loops of Desert Tortoise, you can choose among developed, semideveloped, or tent sites. The campground sits right at the water's edge, and most sites have great views of the lake.

Pass by the Scute Loop, the first turn along Desert Tortoise Road. These sites are at the tail end of Sunset Cove, a narrow inlet that turns dry when the water level is low. Instead, turn into the Bajada Loop. On the right, look for site 133, just below the road across from the restrooms. This walk-in site claims its own promontory, and the water is just a short scramble down a rocky, steep slope. Your view from here looks down the cove toward the lake, and you may feel like your tent is a tiny castle. Turn at the restroom and head uphill around

Spring poppies bejewel the slopes above Lake Pleasant.

KEY INFORMATION

CONTACT: 928-501-1710, tinyurl.com
/deserttortoisecampground

OPEN: Year-round

SITES: 76 (10 walk-in tent sites)

EACH SITE HAS: Picnic table, fire ring,
ramada, some have water spigots, some
have electrical hookups

ASSIGNMENT: First-come, first-served or
by reservation

REGISTRATION: Purchase daily and
annual passes at the park entrance
station; use self-pay station when
entrance station closed

AMENITIES: Flush toilets, hot showers,
water spigots, boat ramp, picnic shelters,
dump station, interpretive activities and
programs, water at visitor center, drinking
fountains, group sites, campground host,
wheelchair-accessible sites, firewood

PARKING: At campsites or group parking
area for walk-in sites

FEE: $12–$30/night; $8 online-
reservation fee

ELEVATION: 1,700'

RESTRICTIONS:

PETS: On leash only

FIRES: In fire rings only

ALCOHOL: Permitted

VEHICLES: 50-foot length limit; 2 vehicles/
site; off-road driving prohibited

QUIET HOURS: 10 p.m.–6 a.m.

OTHER: 14-day stay limit; 8-person
limit/site; 2 tents/site; state fishing
permits required; glass bottles prohibited;
loaded firearms prohibited; removal of
vegetation prohibited

the one-way loop to reach the highest part of the peninsula, where glimpses of the lake open into an impressive panorama. As you round the loop you come to two of our favorite sites, 159 and 160. The sites are 50 and 100 feet from the parking, screened by paloverde, mesquite, and other desert scrub brush. If you brought along your kayak or canoe, you can portage down to the shore and begin exploring the lake right from your campsite.

Water and electricity seem incongruous at walk-in tent sites, but the entire loop is developed and will allow you to camp in luxury if you choose. (If you have a portable evaporative cooler, it might almost make summer camping here bearable.) Continuing around the loop, you will come to another parking area for two more tent sites, 161 and 162. They have incredible views of the lake, but also of each other, so they would make a good group site. If you didn't bring anything with a plug, continue down Desert Tortoise Road to the Pallet Loop. After passing the campground host's site, you'll find six sites on your left. While not well screened from each other, they're just fine if you like an open feeling and a terrific view. Below the road on your right are five more tent sites, 166–170. Park at the shared parking lot and climb down a few steps to reach them. The first four are all in a row, cascading down toward the water, with site 169 the closest to the water's edge. The fifth, 170, is off by itself just below the road.

All sites have a small shade ramada, but be forewarned that the summer months are scorchers, and loud voices as well as loud engines carry well over the water. On the other hand, if you've got a good sleeping bag for chilly nights, midwinter can offer perfect days for exploring one of the several hikes around the lake. You're also welcome to dry camp anywhere along the shoreline. If you continue down Desert Tortoise Road, don't speed, because the pavement disappears right into the water. People who've come to scuba-dive often park or camp here, making it easy to get their equipment into the water.

Boating and fishing are, naturally, the primary activities on the lake. The lake hosts more than a dozen species of fish, including introduced species such as tilapia and white crappie. You'll find three boat ramps, one of them 10 lanes wide, and all provide ample parking. Don't have a boat? Don't worry, Scorpion Bay Marina offers boat, Jet Ski, kayak, and paddleboard rentals. It also has a floating restaurant with lake views. Pleasant Harbor Marina, a privately owned business outside of the park, also offers a restaurant, store, and sightseeing cruises.

Check the events calendar online or at the visitor center for information and details about upcoming ranger-led hikes and kayak/canoe tours, children's activities, educational programs, and fishing tournaments. The Desert Outdoor Center, located at the southeastern edge of the lake, is an old guest ranch that can be reserved for educational programs, weddings, and business meetings; contact them for dates for the next stargazing party or guided hiking tour open to the public. Lake Pleasant was formed by damming the Agua Fria River, which feeds into the lake from the northeast. At the visitor center you can learn more about seasonal closures of the Agua Fria inlet for nesting bald eagles, as well as see local critters, including a live desert tortoise, Gila monster, and a tarantula.

Desert Tortoise Campground

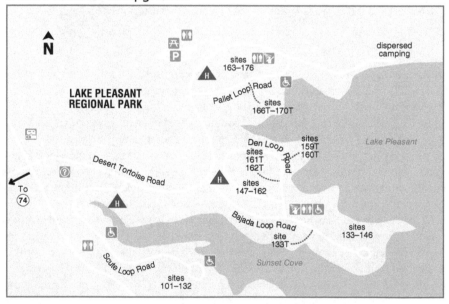

GETTING THERE

From Phoenix, take I-17 north to Exit 223 for Carefree Highway (AZ 74). Turn left and drive northwest 11.2 miles to Castle Hot Springs Road. Turn right and head north 2.2 miles to Lake Pleasant Access Road. Turn right and drive 0.3 mile to the park entrance station. Continue 0.45 mile to South Park Road. Turn right and drive south 0.27 mile to Desert Tortoise Road.

GPS COORDINATES N33° 51.655' W112° 18.492'

16

Hazlett Hollow Campground

Beauty ★★★ Privacy ★★★★ Spaciousness ★★★ Quiet ★★★ Security ★★★ Cleanliness ★★

See the handiwork of the Civilian Conservation Corps in the stone walls and steps leading up to restored Adirondack shelters.

Wend your way north up I-17 through the Aqua Fria River valley from Phoenix to Flagstaff, and even before you've left the saguaros behind, the rugged Bradshaw Mountains rise to the west. Tucked secretively in the forested interior is the thriving hamlet of Crown King. Named after the Crowned King mine, the town once served as the center of a bustling mining district and today is a popular tourist destination and summer retreat.

Leave the highway at the signs for the Horsethief Basin Recreation Area and pass through tiny Cleator. As you begin to climb into the hills, take note of the road. In the late 1800s, naysayers doubted entrepreneur Frank Murphy could build a railroad through these rocky mountains to the valley of Mayer. But Murphy made it happen: completed in 1904, it successfully transported more than $1 million worth of ore. The rails were taken up in 1927, but the gentle grade and narrow rock-cut passages of "Murphy's Impossible Railroad" remain. At the hairpin turns, look for the areas where the train was switched onto a spur, backed up the next slope, switched onto another spur, then pulled forward again—the process that gave us the word *switchback*.

Camp in classic CCC style, with rustic stonework and an Adirondack shelter.

KEY INFORMATION

CONTACT: 928-443-8000, tinyurl.com
/hazletthollow

OPEN: May 1–October 1

SITES: 15

EACH SITE HAS: Adirondack shelter, picnic
table, fire ring, upright grill

ASSIGNMENT: First-come, first-served;
no reservations

REGISTRATION: Self-register on-site

AMENITIES: Vault toilets, water spigots

PARKING: At campsites

FEE: $10/night, $5/additional vehicle

ELEVATION: 6,000'

RESTRICTIONS:

PETS: On leash only

FIRES: In fire rings only

ALCOHOL: Permitted

VEHICLES: 32-foot length limit; ATVs
and motorbikes prohibited, high
clearance recommended

QUIET HOURS: 10 p.m.–6 a.m.

OTHER: 14-day stay limit; bear-country food-
storage restrictions; firearms prohibited;
10-person limit/site; checkout 2 p.m.

Near the now-collapsed railway tunnel, you'll turn through a narrow passage (watch out for ATVs) and suddenly find yourself "downtown" among the pines. Turn right to check out the Crown King Saloon, heroically saved from several historic fires even as other buildings burned. During one early incident, quick-thinking miners reduced the potential flammability of the saloon by drinking its entire contents. The upstairs rooms from its bordello days are now available for legitimate lodging. Load up with homemade fudge from the James P. Cleator General Store or have some Thrifty ice cream at the Rocky Road Sweet Stop; then continue down Forest Road 52 for 7 miles to Hazlett Hollow. Travel gets rougher past Crown King, and high clearance is required. If you prefer to camp on your own piece of mountain, you'll find several dispersed camping spots among the boulders and pines along the road.

On your way to Horsethief Basin, you climb higher into clearings affording you grand vistas across the mountains all the way to Phoenix. Outlaws based here once stole horses from Phoenix, changed their brands in the remote valley, sold them in Prescott, and then repeated the process headed in the other direction. The picturesque cabin on your right as you reach the recreation area is available for rent from the U.S. Forest Service as part of their Rooms with a View program. Just up the road opposite the cabin is Horsethief Lake, stocked with largemouth bass, sunfish, and catfish. For a nice short hike, walk across the dam and follow a footpath around the small lake.

As you pull into the campground, look for the handiwork of the Civilian Conservation Corps in the stone walls and steps leading up to restored Adirondack shelters. There are no purpose-made tent pads, but only site 15 lacks a good spot. To experience camping as it was in the 1940s, you can always set up your cot in the shelter. Horsethief Basin Recreation Area was originally built by the City of Phoenix as a summer retreat to help prevent the seasonal exodus from the valley of the sun.

Set in a small, steep valley, the scrub oak and ponderosas provide screening and shade. The sites on the outside of the loop are more private and well separated. Site 14 at the end of the loop has a nice layout with large tenting areas and a level parking tab. Sites 12 and 13 sit very close together and would accommodate two families or a group. Our favorites are sites

6, 7, and 9, with no close neighbors and shelters facing the woods. For sites without steps, choose one inside the loop, but beware of rattlesnakes down in the wash.

Technically ATVs and motorbikes are prohibited in the Horsethief Basin Recreation Area and Hazlett Hollow Campground, but they're a primary form of transportation as well as recreation in this area. Folks camping in the forest sometimes drive through the campground to use the facilities. The campground is not hosted, and it shows some signs of wear and tear, but has plenty of charm to compensate.

A mile farther on is Kentuck Springs, a campground that's been converted to day use. FR 52 climbs steeply past this point, but persevere to the historic Horsethief fire lookout tower, where on a clear day you can see all the way from Phoenix's South Mountain to Flagstaff's San Francisco Peaks. For more information about the local history, contact the Crown King Historical Society.

There's a lot of great hiking around the southern Bradshaws, so check in with the U.S. Forest Service to find out more about Algonquin, Castle Creek, Horsethief Canyon, East Fort, and other trails. For a civilized touch to your experience, head back into Crown King for a gourmet surf-and-turf meal at The Mill at Crown King, a restaurant where the centerpiece is the massive ore-crushing stamp mill from the old Gladiator Mine; then join the crowd at the Crown King Saloon & Cafe for a drink and some live music.

Hazlett Hollow Campground

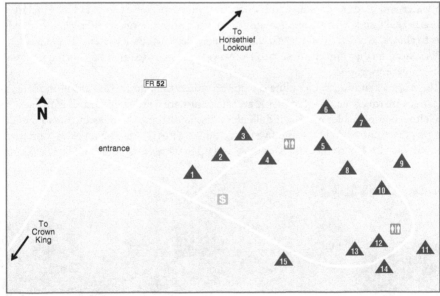

GETTING THERE

From Crown King, take FR 52 southeast 7 miles to the campground.

GPS COORDINATES N34° 10.222' W112° 17.237'

⚶ Ironwood Campground

Beauty ★★★★ Privacy ★★★★ Spaciousness ★★★★★ Quiet ★★★★ Security ★★★ Cleanliness ★★★★

This desert landscape is surprisingly green with towering saguaros, fiery ocotillos, and sage-barked paloverde trees.

McDowell Mountain Regional Park's 21,099 acres make it one of the largest parks in the Maricopa County Parks System. Although only 45 minutes from the Phoenix airport, you might believe that you have stepped back in time in this Sonoran Desert oasis. Located in the lower Verde River basin, this desert landscape is surprisingly green with towering saguaros, fiery ocotillos, and sage-barked paloverde trees, all surrounded by distant mountain ranges. Expect the evenings to be quiet except for the eerie yipping of coyotes nearby, or the light steps of a deer or javelina passing through the campground.

When you arrive, first stop in at the visitor center. Here you will find maps, gifts and souvenirs, educational displays, and refreshments. Be sure to check out the schedule of events, including fitness hikes, live animal presentations, stargazing, or even archery tutorials. Pick up an interpretive brochure for the North Trail Self-Guided Tour, an easy 3 miles that is one of the most popular hikes in the park.

You will pass 76-site E. I. Rowland Campground, accommodating vehicles up to 45 feet with water and electric hookups and a nature-themed play area for the kids (including a cool rattlesnake slide). This campground was named after the man who reclassified federal lands to allow the creation of the Maricopa County Regional Park System. To get away from the RVs, head farther into the desert to Ironwood, a picnic area that has been converted to a tent-only campground.

There are 14 sites here, including one group site in the middle that accommodates 4–6 tents. Because this is a converted picnic area, the sites are a little haphazard, with a few random leftover picnic tables making it difficult to distinguish the boundaries. Sites 1 and 2, for example, share one parking tab and five picnic tables. Sites 6–9 are on an extra loop road so they may see a bit less traffic. Site 10 is large and open with a great view of Four Peaks and is

A green season in the Valley of the Sun

KEY INFORMATION

CONTACT: 480-471-0173, tinyurl.com
/ironwoodcampground

OPEN: Year-round

SITES: 13

EACH SITE HAS: Picnic table, fire ring

ASSIGNMENT: By reservation

REGISTRATION: Purchase daily and annual
passes at the visitor center; self-register
on-site when office is closed

AMENITIES: Flush toilets, hot showers, water
spigots, day-use ramadas, nature trails,
dump station, amphitheater, drinking fountains, group sites, firewood, wheelchair-
accessible sites, playground at E. I. Rowland
Campground; pay phone at visitor center

PARKING: At campsites

FEE: $22/night; $8 online-reservation fee

ELEVATION: 1,765'

RESTRICTIONS:

PETS: On leash only

FIRES: In fire rings only

ALCOHOL: Permitted

VEHICLES: No length limit

QUIET HOURS: 10 p.m.–6 a.m.

OTHER: 14-day stay limit; 2 tents/site unless
group site; 8-person limit/site; discharging of
firearms prohibited; firewood gathering
prohibited; check-in 1 p.m.; checkout noon

directly across from the restrooms. You really can't go wrong with any of the sites, which are screened by dense cholla, paloverde, and scrubby mesquite; just be sure to pitch your tent in the designated areas and not in the temptingly sandy wash. This campground still seems to be a hidden gem, less used than other Phoenix-area parks, so you should be able to reserve a spot for most weekends and may even get the campground to yourself on a weekday.

McDowell Mountain Regional Park also offers three types of group campgrounds—one for up to 30 RVs with flush toilets, hot water showers, and covered ramadas; one for horse camping or larger groups; and a more primitive area for youth groups. The 88 first-come, first-served picnic sites handle the day-use traffic.

The McDowell Mountains are made up of the oldest rocks in the area—metamorphic rocks from around 1,745 million years ago. The highest point (4,034') overlooks the park from the adjoining Scottsdale McDowell Sonoran Preserve. In many areas of the park, you'll have postcard views of the Four Peaks—more than 7,000 feet tall and home to North America's only active amethyst mine—and the Mazatzal Mountains in the distance. This beautiful landscape was home to the Hohokam Indians 2,000 years ago, and several Hohokam hunting and gathering sites can be found in the park.

Ironwood trees are only found in the Sonoran Desert and are prized for the durability of their wood. Look for purple blossoms in May and June. You'll see evidence of the 1995 lightning-caused Rio Fire which burned 23,000 acres, including a significant swath of the park. Although fires are a natural feature of the desert, approximately 80 years will pass before the vegetation is fully recovered, so $44,000 was raised to give nature a hand replanting native trees and cacti in the park.

The mountains are named after Civil War General Irvin McDowell, who visited Camp McDowell, later named Fort McDowell, once in 1863; a hundred years later the first 627 acres were purchased to create McDowell Mountain Regional Park. Today, the park boasts over 50 miles of multiuse trails of all lengths for hikers, bikers, and equestrians. Many visitors to the park are mountain bikers enjoying the challenging diversity of terrain, but if you want to take a more leisurely approach look for the designated hike-only trails. The regional park system connects with numerous additional trails in the Fountain Hills McDowell Mountain Preserve and the Scottsdale McDowell Sonoran Preserve.

The park hosts annual competitions and events, such as the equestrian endurance ride, Dawn-to-Dusk mountain bike rides, and duathlons (triathletes need not apply—there's no swimming here). The McDowell Competitive Track offers 15 miles of challenging trails for runners, bikers, and equestrians.

Don't have your own bicycle or horse? You can rent mountain bikes from vendors in Fountain Hills or time in the saddle at the Stables at Fort McDowell. You could even take a tour by Segway. Adding a surreal touch to your desert visit, just 4 miles away is Fountain Hills, home of the world's tallest free-standing jet fountain. The fountain runs every hour on the hour from 9 a.m. to 9 p.m., can reach 560 feet, and when illuminated is easily visible to confused airline passengers flying into Phoenix. On St. Patrick's Day, the fountain turns green. Take the steep 1.2-mile hike up Lousely Hill near Ironwood Campground for a view of the fountain from the park. For additional information about nearby attractions, see profile 22, The Point Campground, page 79.

Ironwood Campground

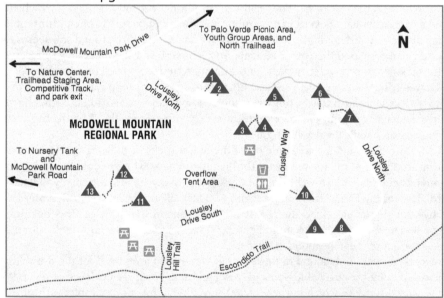

GETTING THERE

From Phoenix, take Loop 202 east to AZ 87. Continue northeast for 11.5 miles to Shea Boulevard. Travel west on Shea Boulevard 0.6 mile to Saguaro Boulevard. Turn right and drive north 4 miles to Fountain Hills Boulevard. Turn right and drive north 5.5 miles to the park entrance. Turn left into the park.

GPS COORDINATES N33° 42.710' W111° 42.129'

Lawrence Crossing Campground

Beauty ★★★★ Privacy ★★★ Spaciousness ★★★ Quiet ★★★ Security ★★★★ Cleanliness ★★★★★

Wet Beaver Creek runs clear and strong below Sedona-red bluffs.

Any property near cool, rushing water in arid Arizona is prime real estate, so it's no surprise that Lawrence Crossing Campground fills up on weekends throughout the year. Six sites are cradled along Wet Beaver Creek, which runs clear and strong below Sedona-red bluffs. Arizona sycamores, cottonwoods, and junipers line the creekbed, shading the chuckling stream and most of the campsites. This is one of the few remaining places where you can camp along this perennial watercourse; after flash floods in Arkansas killed at least 20 campers in 2010, all federal campsites in flood plains were evaluated for safety. Lawrence Crossing passed muster, but the popular Beaver Creek Campground nearby was converted to day use. Much of Wet Beaver Creek also runs within the Wet Beaver Wilderness, where camping is prohibited.

All six sites are just a short walk from the parking area and pit toilets. Sites 1–3 line up along the creek and share a trail from the parking lot. Shady site 1, farthest in, might be the pick of the lot, although there's little screening between 1, 2, and 3. Lawrence Crossing, the old ford across the creek which gives the area its name, lies between sites 4 and 5. Private site 6 is on higher ground and the farthest from the creek, although none of the sites are out of earshot of the water. A small ditch between the creek and the campground provides water to local farmers, while its berm helps prevent the campground from flooding.

Marble-barked sycamores frame the old ford on Wet Beaver Creek.

KEY INFORMATION

CONTACT: 928-203-7500, tinyurl.com /lawrencecrossing

OPEN: Year-round

SITES: 6

EACH SITE HAS: Picnic table, fire ring with grill

ASSIGNMENT: First-come, first-served; no reservations

REGISTRATION: Not required

AMENITIES: Pit toilets

PARKING: Designated area

FEE: None

ELEVATION: 3,800'

RESTRICTIONS:

PETS: On leash only

FIRES: In fire rings only

ALCOHOL: Permitted

VEHICLES: N/A

QUIET HOURS: Not specified

OTHER: 14-day stay limit; discharging of firearms prohibited; firewood gathering prohibited; horses prohibited; 8-person limit/site

Marcus J. Lawrence, a former owner of the V Bar V Ranch, was rumored to be a gambler and a bit of a rake—rumors which may have held some truth, as he was murdered by an acquaintance in a jealous rage in 1938. His mother used his life insurance policies to build a hospital in Cottonwood and improve the ford at Beaver Creek in his honor. Don't plan on driving it yourself, however, as the road is no longer passable, and the campground is not accessible from the east despite what your GPS may tell you.

Wet Beaver Creek is spring-fed, and its level fluctuates with the snowmelt and rain runoff from higher ground near Flagstaff. The stream is regularly stocked with trout, and the campground is stocked with regulars who return most weekends to cast a hopeful line. November is the most popular month of all, when the sycamores' broad leaves change colors. Summers can still be hot here although the creek provides opportunities to cool off.

If you find Lawrence Crossing full or too primitive, check out nearby Clear Creek Campground along AZ 260. Clear Creek Campground offers 18 small, developed sites with picnic tables, a campground host, and a group area. The campground sits near Clear Creek, but you won't hear the babble of water the way you do at Lawrence Crossing.

Just up Forest Road 121, Beaver Creek Day-Use Picnic Site is available for more creekside play and fishing. From the picnic area you can follow any of the many paths down to the creek to reach private fishing spots or cool swimming holes. Just west on FR 618, turn at the historic Beaver Creek Ranger Station for the trailhead to access the Wet Beaver Creek Wilderness. The Bell Trail 13, Apache Maid Trail 15, and White Mesa Trail 86 provide 25 miles of splendid hiking in and around Wet Beaver Creek Canyon.

East on FR 618 is the V Bar V Heritage site, the largest petroglyph site in the Verde Valley. Thought to have been scribed by the Sinagua people, this mysterious aggregation of ancient signs had one use still apparent today, as a solar calendar. Two protruding rocks cast parallel shadows, creating a shaft of sunlight that spotlights particular petroglyphs marking the winter and summer solstice, and perhaps other milestones such as planting and harvest times. A $5-per-vehicle fee (or a Red Rock Pass) and a short walk get you to the petroglyphs, but leave the pooch behind since pets are not allowed.

From Lawrence Crossing it's a quick trip to Montezuma Well, a natural limestone sink that receives more than 1 million gallons of 75°F water daily from warm underground streams. Because of this the well has developed its own unique ecology; it teems with leeches, shrimplike amphipods, water scorpions, and algae. Thousands of years ago, the Sinagua irrigated their crops by diverting the water from the well, and it still provides water to local farmers. The eponymous Aztec emperor never set foot here, but you can learn more about the Sinagua by traveling a bit farther south and visiting the beautifully pre-served cliff dwellings at Montezuma Castle National Monument.

If you need supplies, you can find almost anything in nearby Camp Verde, including the world's largest Kokopelli, a 32-foot, five-ton tribute to the flute-playing fertility figure. Venture a bit farther into historic downtown Cottonwood's several tasting rooms to sample vintages from Arizona's fastest-growing wine region. For other area details see the Powell Springs and Manzanita profiles (pages 30 and 82, respectively).

Lawrence Crossing Campground

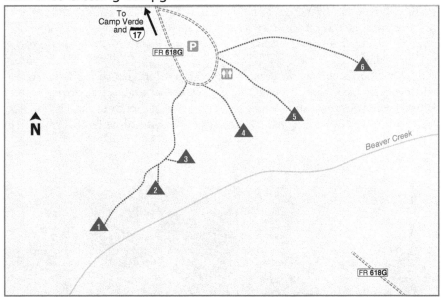

GETTING THERE

From Camp Verde, take I-17 north to FR 618 (Exit 298). Turn right and head east 2 miles to FR 121. Turn right and drive southwest 0.5 mile to FR 121A (FR 618G). Turn left and drive south for 0.25 mile to the campground.

GPS COORDINATES N34° 39.226' W111° 44.022'

⛺ Lost Dutchman State Park Campground

Beauty ★★★★ Privacy ★★★ Spaciousness ★★★ Quiet ★★★ Security ★★★★ Cleanliness ★★★★★

Each campsite has a postcard-perfect backdrop of magnificent red saguaro-studded crags.

Legend has it that Jacob "The Dutchman" Waltz found gold while prospecting in the rugged Superstition Mountains. On his deathbed he revealed the location of his mine to two close friends, but they were unable to find it. Thousands have since gone into these mountains in search of their fortunes, and some have died trying; the Dutchman's treasure remains hidden today, even though maps to the possible location are on display at the Superstition Mountain Museum in Apache Junction. There may be no more truth to the tale than to Waltz's nickname (he was actually German), but I remember coming to the Supes for the first time as a teenager convinced I was the one who would find the lost gold. Instead I discovered an abiding love for the desert.

The Superstition Mountain Wilderness is a rugged desert gem right on the edge of the sprawling Phoenix metro area. Multiple hiking and horseback-riding trails meander through the 160,000-acre wilderness stretching east of the city and south of the historic Apache Trail. Each campsite at Lost Dutchman State Park has a postcard-perfect backdrop of these

Rumors of gold still haunt the Superstition Mountains.

KEY INFORMATION

CONTACT: 480-982-4485, 877-697-2757, azstateparks.com/lost-dutchman

OPEN: Year-round

SITES: 134 (3 walk-in tent sites)

EACH SITE HAS: Picnic table, upright grill

ASSIGNMENT: Reservations available online and strongly encouraged except for over-flow nonelectric sites; reservations also accepted for group sites and ramadas

REGISTRATION: Purchase daily and annual passes at the park office; self-register on-site after hours

AMENITIES: Flush toilets, hot showers, water spigots, picnic shelters, day-use ramadas, nature trails, dump station, amphitheater, interpretive activities and programs, guided hikes, interpretive center, drinking fountains, group sites, campground host, resident park manager, recycling

PARKING: At campsites, group parking for walk-in sites

FEE: $20–$30/night, $15/additional vehicle; $5 online-reservation fee; $7 day use

ELEVATION: 2,000'

RESTRICTIONS:

PETS: On leash only

FIRES: No ground fires

ALCOHOL: Permitted

VEHICLES: No length limit; 2 vehicles/site; motorized vehicles and bicycles prohibited in the Superstition Wilderness

QUIET HOURS: 9 p.m.–8 a.m.

OTHER: 14-day stay limit; firearms prohibited; firewood gathering prohibited; 12-person limit/site; 15-person limit for groups hiking in the wilderness; generator hours 8 a.m.–9 p.m.; day use closes at 10 p.m.

---

magnificent red saguaro–studded crags, and the park makes a good fall-to-spring base camp for your own prospecting trip.

When you first pull into the park, be sure to stop inside the visitor center to learn more about the area. If you're interested in bird-watching, pick up a birding list and point your binoculars toward the small pool along the native plant trail. Among the sparrows you may catch a glimpse of a curve-billed thrasher, a roadrunner, or a gaggle of Gambel's quail. Walk the short trail to learn the names of the plants that thrive in this desert.

Continuing into the park, a left turn takes you to the day-use areas, a right turn to the campground. Skip the first loop; you'll find sites with better screening, more privacy, and a nicer spot to pitch your tent just ahead. Heading down the road, take the second left to enter the 1–15 loop. These first few sites are our favorites since mature paloverde trees shade them. Because this loop only has pull-in tab parking, you are less likely to have a big RV next door. If you end up on a pull-through loop, check out sites 59–70, which are separated by thick brush.

If you really want privacy, you can also stay at one of the three walk-in hiker/biker campsites, located along the Discovery Interpretive Trail. You'll be near the Siphon Draw Trailhead, making these perfect sites for an early start to your own hike. They even come with their own bird feeder and bath. A mountain bike trail circumnavigates the entire campground.

You could hike in the Superstitions every weekend for years and never see it all. This is lowland Sonoran desert, with its signature saguaro and cholla cactus, but you'll also find tree-shaded streams and deep-canyon swimming holes hidden in these hills. From the campground, you can hike the 4-mile round-trip straight up to the towering cliffs that back-drop the campsites and into Siphon Draw Canyon. The final 2 miles of the hike up to the summit at the Flatiron has been called one of the hardest climbs in the Valley of the Sun—2,800 steep and rocky feet up an unmaintained trail. Just north of the state park is the easy

3-mile Massacre Grounds Trail, which leads you through a surreal cholla forest to the scene of a brutal 1848 confrontation between Mexican prospectors and Apaches.

Summer temperatures regularly reach triple digits, so plan your trip for cooler weather. Winter days average in the 60s, but the sun is still intense, so wear your hat and sunscreen. Be sure to bring plenty of water with you in any season, and if you decide to try for that fabled gold, remember that treasure hunting requires a permit issued through Tonto National Forest.

The Superstitions are also popular with rock climbers, especially at Weaver's Needle. This unique rock formation, created by long-ago volcanic activity, rises 4,550 feet in elevation and can be summited by experienced technical climbers. For a spectacular camping experience, haul your tent to the top of the Needle and spend the night on top of the world. Weaver's Needle can be seen from many vantage points in the Superstitions and is accessed by the Peralta Trail, off of US 60 east of Apache Junction.

Just outside the park, you can tour the old mines of Goldfield, a very productive gold mining region that some have suggested was the actual location of the Lost Dutchman Mine. Continue on AZ 88 to drive the Historic Apache Trail past Canyon Lake to the ghost town of Tortilla Flat, population six. You can cowboy up at the bar in the Superstition Saloon on the saddle barstools and add your dollar bill to the wallpaper of greenbacks posted by tourists. Be sure to try the prickly pear ice cream, a sweet concoction that might sweeten your feelings toward cactus.

Lost Dutchman State Park Campground

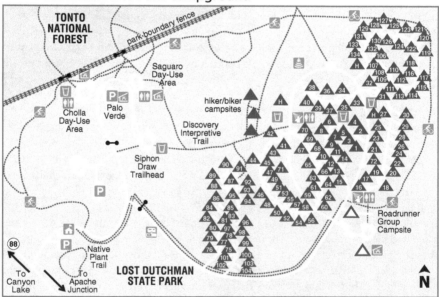

GETTING THERE

From Phoenix, take US 60 east to AZ 88. Turn left and head north 5 miles to the park entrance.

GPS COORDINATES N33° 27.863' W111° 28.922'

20

Lower Wolf Creek Campground

Beauty ★★★ Privacy ★★★ Spaciousness ★★★ Quiet ★★ Security ★★★ Cleanliness ★★★

Gambel oaks and walnuts become a patchwork of gold and copper.

The Prescott Basin lies to the south and west of the burgeoning community of Prescott and encompasses 59,000 acres of the Prescott National Forest. Mixed-conifer forest covers much of the land, but stands of oak and stretches of pinyon pine and juniper woodland are also common. A wildland-urban interface area, this part of Arizona provides days of scenic drives and plenty of camping, hiking, and sightseeing opportunities.

You'll find several campgrounds in the Prescott Basin, each with its own appeal, but Lower Wolf Creek will best suit most tent campers. The campground is in a creek-carved valley, in a stand of ponderosa pine, fir, Arizona walnut, and Gambel oak. This is an old Civilian Conservation Corps camp, and the stone masonry picnic tables add rustic appeal. Boulders decorate the pine needle–strewn ground and provide extra screening in some sites. The Senator Highway which brings you most of the way here from Prescott is a well-graded dirt road passable by passenger cars in dry weather.

Lower Wolf Creek Campground sprawls along both sides of Forest Road 97. Pull into the south entrance and the host and sites 1–5 are to your left. Sites 1 and 2 are off a spur road and may have the occasional ATV enthusiast roaring past. We liked the feel of site 3, and site 4 sits picturesquely in a nest of boulders; both are close enough to the creek to hear it clearly when it's running.

A crisp fall day is a beautiful time to camp at Lower Wolf Creek.

KEY INFORMATION

CONTACT: 928-443-8000, tinyurl.com /lowerwolfcreek

OPEN: May 1–October 31

SITES: 20

EACH SITE HAS: Picnic table, fire ring

ASSIGNMENT: First-come, first-served; reservations accepted for group site

REGISTRATION: Self-register on-site

AMENITIES: Vault toilets, campground host, firewood

PARKING: At designated areas

FEE: $10/night, $5/additional vehicle

ELEVATION: 6,000'

RESTRICTIONS:

PETS: On leash only

FIRES: In fire rings only

ALCOHOL: Permitted

VEHICLES: 40-foot length limit; 2 vehicles/site

QUIET HOURS: 10 p.m.–6 a.m

OTHER: 14-day stay limit; firearms prohibited; no drinking water available; 10-person limit/site

Go back past the host and sites 8–16 trail to the west, following the line of the dry creekbed. If you'd like a little more solitude, head down to the sites at the end of the line. Site 14 is up a flight of stone steps from a walled, single-car pullout and offers a spacious, sandy tent area set back from the picnic table, but may be hot on a sunny summer day. There's a glimpse of a view through the ponderosas and oaks in site 15, plus a nice tent spot. Private site 16 backs up to a richly forested area of the creekbed, but is so close to a marked flood zone, it's probably best for folks sleeping in their vehicle.

The remaining sites lie on the north side of FR 97, across from the western end of the main loop. If you like the high ground, head for sites 19 and 20, uphill from the parking and overlooking the rest of the campground. Site 19 has a couple of good, partially screened tent spots. Just up the road to the east is Upper Wolf Creek, a group campground that can accommodate up to 100 people. Reservations are required and can be made online at recreation.gov or by calling 877-444-6777.

Summer visitors from the low desert will find it pleasantly cool here, with temperatures averaging at least 20° cooler than in Phoenix. Ask the camp host about hiking along the creek, and remember to prepare for sudden thunderstorms during July–September. Lower Wolf Creek shines in fall; in September and October, the Gambel oaks and walnuts become a patchwork of gold and copper.

For a nice 8-mile loop hike through ponderosa and fir, drive north on Senator Highway to the Groom Creek Equestrian Camp. Park at the trailhead across the street from the campground. The Groom Creek Loop Trail 307 will take you past the fire lookout tower, which you can climb if manned and see all the way to the San Francisco Peaks and the Mogollon Rim. Watch your step along the path, as you'll likely share the trail with horses as well as bicyclists.

If the campground is full, or just too crowded for you, feel free to find your own private piece of the forest. Several designated dispersed camping sites are available along FR 74 to the west of the campground. You may also continue south down the Senator Highway to reach additional dispersed sites. A metal post that proclaims DISPERSED CAMPSITE marks each one. You'll find a fire pit, but usually no other amenities. There's no fee, of course, and you may stay in a dispersed site for 7 days in any 30-day period.

If you have the time, loop back to Prescott by going south on the Senator Highway to Walker Road. The road winds precariously through the forest, past vacation homes, and eventually up to Lynx Lake. Spend the day trout fishing on this 55-acre lake, rent a kayak from the Lynx Lake Store and Marina, or stroll the paved lakeshore path and watch the cormorants hold their wings out to dry. A flash of black and white in the distance could be an osprey or a bald eagle, or closer at hand, a tiny bridled titmouse.

For a fun four-wheel-drive adventure, take Senator Highway south to Palace Station, an old stagecoach station between Phoenix and Prescott. Built in 1873, Palace Station is now listed on the National Register of Historic Places. Continue into the Bradshaw Mountains to Crown King, an old mining town turned tourist destination. For more details about the Crown King area, see profile 16, Hazlett Hollow Campground (page 61).

Lower Wolf Creek Campground

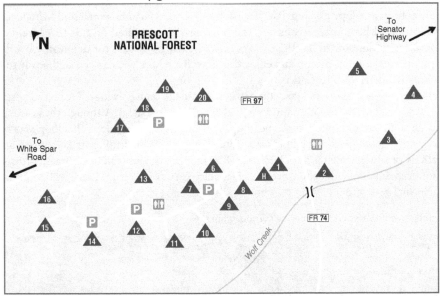

GETTING THERE

From Prescott, take Senator Highway (Mt. Vernon Avenue) south 6 miles to FR 97. Turn right and drive west 1.25 miles to the campground entrance. Turn left into the campground.

Alternate route (high-clearance vehicles only): From Prescott, take US 89 (White Spar Road) south 6 miles to FR 97. Turn left and drive east 5.1 miles to the campground. Turn right into the campground.

GPS COORDINATES N34° 27.303' W112° 27.623'

21

Mingus Mountain Campground

Beauty ★★★★ Privacy ★★★ Spaciousness ★★★ Quiet ★★★ Security ★★★ Cleanliness ★★★★

Take your camp chair for a short stroll to the edge and settle in to contemplate the never-ending views.

A sinuous section of AZ 89A, designated the Mingus Mountain Scenic Road, snakes its way from Jerome across the Black Hills toward Prescott. These hills have been mined since prehistoric times, and if you look closely, piles of telltale tailings will reveal where fortunes were made and (far more often) lost. Where the road passes over the hills' summit, turn at the picnic area onto Forest Road 104, the twisting but manageable dirt road up to Mingus Mountain. On your way, peruse the Church Meadow Wildlife Area, where you may spot shy pronghorn antelope grazing. Past the Methodist church camp, you'll find Mingus Lake (formerly called Elk Tank). Swimming and boating are prohibited on this tiny lake, but it is stocked with rainbow trout. There is a $5 day-use fee, as there is for the nearby overlook and picnic area. Be sure to stop and enjoy the view; from here you can see all the way to the San Francisco Peaks in Flagstaff.

The first six campsites that you come to constitute the tent-only loop. Our picks here are site 1, with a secret tent spot on the rocky ridge nearby, and site 3. Although these are nice, shady sites, for mountaintop views head up the road to the next loop. This loop was built with electric hookups and drinking water, but due to a 2016 lightning strike, there was no electricity or water available as of late 2018. RVs may be discouraged from braving the road up until repairs are made, and once the electricity is running again, there will be no need for growling generators.

The distant Verde Valley is coolly blue below your campsite.

KEY INFORMATION

CONTACT: 928-567-4121, tinyurl.com
/mingusmountain

OPEN: May–October

SITES: 25

EACH SITE HAS: Picnic table, fire ring;
some have an upright grill

ASSIGNMENT: First-come, first-served;
no reservations

REGISTRATION: Self-register on-site

AMENITIES: Vault toilets, day-use area,
group site

PARKING: At campsites

FEE: $10/night; $5 day use

ELEVATION: 7,500'

RESTRICTIONS:

PETS: On leash only

FIRES: In fire rings only

ALCOHOL: Permitted

VEHICLES: 22-foot length limit

QUIET HOURS: 10 p.m.–6 a.m.

OTHER: 14-day stay limit; no drinking
water available; 10-person limit/site;
checkout 2 p.m.

There were once intended to be level tent pads at each site, but budget cuts took their toll. Although the rocky ground is not ideal, previous campers have taken a hand and most sites will accommodate a tent or two. The expansive feeling and terrific vistas make up for any shortcomings. From sites 6, 8, 10, and 11, take your camp chair for a short stroll to the edge and settle in to contemplate the never-ending view over the Verde Valley to the Secret Mountain Wilderness and the red rocks of Sedona.

At 7,500 feet you'll find the temperature pleasantly cool in the summer. The wind often rises over the mountain and blows across the summit—incentive to stake your tent and one reason hang gliders love this spot. Two Arizona Hang Glider Association cliff launch points are up the road across the vista day-use area. If you prefer to keep your feet on terra firma, the campground makes a good base for exploring the region's numerous hiking trails. The View Point Trail 106 near the Mingus picnic area only *seems* to drop off the cliff, and it makes a moderate 4.25-mile loop hike when combined with North Mingus Trail 105 and 105A. It's especially beautiful in fall when the maples and oaks begin to change. Across AZ 89A in Potato Patch Campground is Woodchute Trail, a mild 8-mile round-trip through designated wilderness to spectacular panoramic views from the north end of Woodchute Mountain.

No trip to the Black Hills is complete without a stop in what was once the "wickedest town in America" and is now the liveliest ghost town you'll ever see. Built by hard-rock miners on the 30° slopes of Cleopatra Hill, precarious Jerome supported one of the most successful mines in the world, generating $1 million a month at its peak. In the 1920s, 15,000 residents made it Arizona's fourth-largest city. The miners' lives were tough; they took pleasure where they could, and the town was filled with saloons, gambling halls, opium dens, and brothels, staying wild well past the taming of the rest of the West. When the mines closed in 1953, the population dwindled to a stubborn 100-or-so folks and Jerome became a ghost town. Artists, entrepreneurs, and hippies realized they could purchase the old bordellos cheaply and, slowly, art galleries, hotels, restaurants, and shops began to open. The government designated the entire town a national historic district in 1967, and today the city is a thriving artist community and a popular tourist destination. Many of the old buildings are rumored to be haunted, and locals embrace the spectral past. You can eat at the Haunted Hamburger or the Asylum or stay at the Ghost City Inn. Around Halloween, you can join the Jerome Historical Society's ghost walk or attend the annual costume ball in the community center, affectionately dubbed "Spook Hall."

Fires and gravity have taken some of the buildings (including the town jail), but most of the remaining structures date from the turn of the last century, and only look as if they're going to give out at any second and tumble down the mountain. Stop by the Jerome Historical Society's Mine Museum and see old mining equipment, gambling goods, and photos of what Jerome looked like in its heyday.

Mingus Mountain Campground

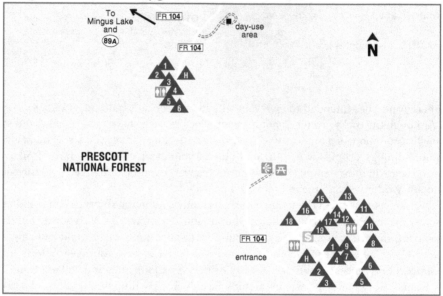

GETTING THERE

From Jerome, take AZ 89A southwest 9 miles uphill to FR 104. Turn left and drive southeast 2.5 miles to the stop sign. Turn right and head 0.5 mile to the campground. Turn left into the campground.

GPS COORDINATES N34° 41.502′ W112° 07.152′

22

The Point Campground

Beauty ★★★★ Privacy ★★★ Spaciousness ★★★★ Quiet ★★ Security ★★ Cleanliness ★★

Transfer your car-camping gear to something that floats.

As the Salt River winds down to the Valley of the Sun, it has carved deep and sometimes spectacular canyons. In the narrow passage between the Mazatzal and Superstition Mountains, the canyon has been dammed to create four deep reservoirs that quench the mighty thirst of Phoenix. Read running upriver, their names form the mnemonic SCAR: Saguaro, Canyon, Apache, and Roosevelt. On Canyon Lake you'll find the unusual camping opportunity of three nicely developed sites with facilities—and no road access at all. Transfer your car camping gear to something that floats a little better and enjoy a night at the Point.

Before you leave, get your Tonto Pass. Canyon Lake is in Tonto National Forest, and you'll have to buy a daily recreation pass. If you plan to camp, get enough passes to cover each day you'll be in the national forest, and if you're bringing a power boat, you may also need a watercraft sticker. More information about the Tonto Pass can be found under Permits and Access in the Introduction (page 8).

Follow the historic Apache Trail as it twists and winds its way through the saguaro-studded canyon. Stop at the overlook just before you begin the final descent to get a bird's-eye view of the lake's main basin, deep-blue water patterned by white wakes. Past the final curve,

A ramada affords precious summer shade at The Point.

KEY INFORMATION

CONTACT: 480-610-3300, tinyurl.com
/thepointcampground

OPEN: Year-round

SITES: 3

EACH SITE HAS: Picnic table, fire ring,
upright grill, ramada

ASSIGNMENT: First-come, first-served;
no reservations

REGISTRATION: Not required; purchase daily
Tonto Pass before arriving

AMENITIES: Composting toilets, boat dock,
emergency phone

PARKING: At Palo Verde Boating Site, Canyon Lake Marina, or Laguna Boating Site

FEE: $8/vehicle; $4/motorized watercraft

ELEVATION: 1,700'

RESTRICTIONS:

PETS: On leash only

FIRES: In fire rings only

ALCOHOL: Permitted

VEHICLES: Access by boat only

QUIET HOURS: 10 p.m.–6 a.m.

OTHER: 14-day stay limit; pack-in/out;
discharging firearms prohibited; no
drinking water; horses, glass containers
prohibited; soaps/detergents prohibited
in lake

look down from the one-lane bridge that spans First Water Cove to see who's fishing the quiet inlet. The lake is routinely stocked with rainbow trout and produces record-breaking largemouth bass. The creased canyon walls form many coves for fish and fishermen to explore.

If you're trailering a boat, you can launch from either the Palo Verde or Laguna boating site. Paddlers might be happier launching from the swimming beach at Acacia Recreation Site, as it's a bit closer to the Point. If you're boatless, Canyon Lake Marina offers rentals ranging from kayaks to pontoon party barges. As you might expect this close to Phoenix, this can be a very crowded lake. On weekends from April through October, it often reaches maximum boating capacity early in the day, so arrive early or be prepared to wait for someone else to pull out.

Across the broad stretch of water from the marina, you'll see boats running at full speed seemingly disappear into the unforgiving cliffs. They're not suicidal; they're actually following the river as it winds its way to the northeast, eventually reaching Horse Mesa Dam on Apache Lake. Your destination lies up this sheer, snaking, stone corridor. The official direction of lake traffic is counterclockwise, but few seem to care, so keep your eyes peeled for distracted ski-boat drivers and Jet Ski cowboys. Canoes and kayaks will be safest sticking to the shoreline, where you're rewarded with the company of great blue herons and curious grebes, and you may even glimpse bighorn sheep on narrow canyon ledges.

Three miles up the lake, three campsites on a headland jutting from the northern shore comprise the Point Campground. The dock can easily accommodate several boats, and a short uphill trail leads to the three sites and restroom building. As the only proper toilet on the upper part of the lake, this sees a lot of day (and some night) use. Each of the three sites has a sizable shade ramada that covers the picnic table as well as a large, flat area to pitch your tent. This was a great idea on someone's part, since the temperature difference between shade and sun can be significant any time of the year. Each site has an upright grill and a fire pit, so be sure to bring the barbecue supplies.

Site 1 is convenient to the dock but could use a little more screening from the restroom foot traffic. Site 3, which sits above and behind the restroom, has plenty of privacy, yet a nice open feeling and great views. Our pick is site 2, farthest from the dock and most secluded. The ground cover is surprisingly dense with mesquite, paloverde trees, brittlebush, jojoba, and cholla, and all three sites are strategically placed so that you can't see your neighbors. In spring, blooming yellow brittlebush, orange globemallow, and purple scorpionweed envelop the sites in color.

The Point Campground is a great place to escape the city, indulge in cool, splashy fun, and spend a night under the stars, but we won't fib to you: there's not a lot of peace or solitude here. The canyon walls amplify the growl of engines day and night, and you won't spend much time out of sight of other people. If you get the chance, come midweek or in the off-season.

The Maricopa County Sheriff's Office, Arizona Game and Fish, and the U.S. Forest Service all police the lake. An emergency call box on the restroom building should bring help if you require it. There's no drinking water, and the campground is pack-in/pack-out, so plan accordingly. Some basic supplies, such as firewood, are available at Canyon Lake Marina, and you can always treat yourself to a meal at the cantina that overlooks the water. Next door is the berth of the *Dolly* steamboat, which chugs on leisurely, narrated cruises around the lake. Check out the Burnt Corral and Cholla profiles (pages 52 and 55, respectively) for more about the canyon lakes and the Apache Trail.

The Point Campground

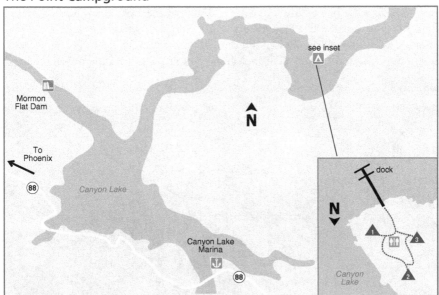

GETTING THERE

From Phoenix, take US 60 east to Idaho Road (Exit 196). Turn left and drive north 2.25 miles to AZ 88. Turn right and head northeast 14.1 miles to Canyon Lake Marina.

GPS COORDINATES (CANYON LAKE MARINA) N33° 32.089' W111° 25.351'

GPS COORDINATES (THE POINT CAMPGROUND) N33° 33.426' W111° 24.679'

⛺ Powell Springs Campground

Beauty ★★★ Privacy ★★★ Spaciousness ★★★ Quiet ★★★ Security ★★★ Cleanliness ★★★★

Wild-grape vines add a touch of green.

Powell Springs is only 15 miles from Arizona's central corridor and I-17, but it feels as if you're in the middle of nowhere. Paved Forest Road 372 brings you up from the junction with AZ 169 through low chaparral, and winds through sandy washes below the Black Hills. The campground is at 5,300 feet elevation but is shaded by a surprising grove of ponderosa pines, along with scrub oak and alligator juniper. Wild-grape vines add a touch of verdant green. The area is peppered with springs and crisscrossed with streambeds, but after years of drought, most run only after heavy rains. Powell Springs still produces clear, fresh water, although the spigot in the campground was locked down after reckless campers broke the pump twice (water was still unavailable at press time). A family of harrier hawks nests annually in the canyon, and they may sweep past you, calling shrilly to one another and swooping dangerously through the trees.

Like so many of Arizona's campgrounds, Powell Springs was built by the Civilian Conservation Corps (CCC) in the 1930s and has the stonework to prove it. The masonry pillar near site 11 may look like a chimney, but we're told it was once the only postal drop for the vicinity, including the nearby town of Cherry. The sites are leveled, and several are raised above the parking areas and surrounded by low stone walls. Most sites have their original fieldstone tables and sunken fire pits, with the addition of upright grills. Erosion is plainly at work, but the CCC nevertheless built well, and the campground is still in good shape.

Powell Springs feels like an isolated oasis.

KEY INFORMATION

CONTACT: 928-567-4121, tinyurl.com/powellspringscampground

OPEN: Year-round when roads are open

SITES: 11

EACH SITE HAS: Picnic table, fire ring, upright grill

ASSIGNMENT: First-come, first-served; no reservations

REGISTRATION: Not required

AMENITIES: Vault toilets; no water

PARKING: At campsites

FEE: None

ELEVATION: 5,300'

RESTRICTIONS:

PETS: On leash only

FIRES: In fire rings only

ALCOHOL: Permitted

VEHICLES: 40-foot length limit; ATVs prohibited

QUIET HOURS: 10 p.m.–6 a.m.

OTHER: 14-day stay limit; firearms and fireworks prohibited; horses prohibited; pack in/pack out; checkout 2 p.m.; 10-person limit/site

The first three sites are well spaced under the tall pines, with morning and evening shade. Sites 4 and 8 are quite close to the camp road and have hearths instead of fire pits. Site 5 is spacious and shady, with generous parking and a large tent spot; this site is sometimes reserved for a host, although it's been a few years since one was in residence (this was still true at press time). Past the modern vault toilets, sites 6 and 7 are open and less shady. The remaining sites back up to the wash that borders the campground. During the spring snowmelt, the wash may be a running stream.

The campground is accessible all year and is well maintained. Some folks stay here long enough to put up hummingbird feeders, and with the location and climate, you can't blame them. Summer evenings cool off here, even when the days are hot; winters are crisp, and occasionally downright cold. Be aware that brief flash floods may occur after heavy monsoon rains and cause washouts on the unpaved camp road.

Leaving camp, head north on FR 372. Shortly before you reach the tiny town of Cherry, you can turn northwest on FR 132, part of the Great Western Trail. This combination route of byways, forest roads, and jeep trails runs from Mexico to Canada through some of the West's most spectacular country; this short-but-rugged section takes you toward Mingus Mountain and the fun and funky town of Jerome (for details see profile 21, Mingus Mountain Campground, page 76). Past this junction, the road turns to dirt, and you're quickly in Cherry, which began life as a stage stop on the route between Prescott (then Fort Whipple) and Camp Verde. It's now a charming little community of summer homes with one bed-and-breakfast and some ghostly remnants of its mining-town past. No services are available.

As you leave Cherry, the road begins its descent toward the Verde River, and the red ramparts of the western Mogollon Rim are visible across the valley. Take your time on this lovely drive down to Camp Verde, where you can explore Arizona's difficult frontier years at Fort Verde State Historical Park, one of General George Crook's headquarters during the Apache Wars. If you'd like to go further back in time, you're very close to Montezuma Castle National Monument, with its beautifully preserved 20-room Sinagua cliff house, and Montezuma Well, a unique geological oasis with life-forms found nowhere else. To spend some time enjoying the Verde, Arizona's only designated Wild and Scenic River, turn west on AZ 260 to Cottonwood and Dead Horse Ranch State Park. The Verde River Greenway, a 6-mile stretch of the river, offers a rare cottonwood-and-willow riparian forest habitat, and you'll find terrific wildlife-spotting and bird-watching opportunities here. For canoeists and kayakers, there's also a paddle trail along this stretch of the river.

Powell Springs Campground

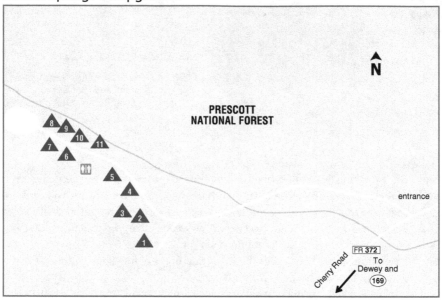

GETTING THERE

From Dewey, take AZ 169 northeast 9.5 miles to FR 372 (Cherry Road). Turn left and continue north 4 miles to the campground entrance. Turn left into the campground.

GPS COORDINATES N34° 34.662′ W112° 03.920′

24

Upper Pinal Campground

Beauty ★★★★ Privacy ★★★★ Spaciousness ★★★ Quiet ★★★★ Security ★★★ Cleanliness ★★★

You won't see your neighbors from any of the sites.

Only 10 miles of smooth gravel roads separate Pinal Mountain Recreation Area from the mining meccas of Globe and Miami, but the atmosphere is a world apart. At 7,500 feet, the trees are tall and the air fresh. It's delightfully cooler than in the desert below, which persuaded many early miners to make the trek to homes up here after hard, hot workdays in the mines. Signal Peak (7,812') was used by the U.S. Army as a heliograph station, allowing frontier commanders to communicate for miles by reflecting sunlight off of mirrors. Today the peaks are topped with a multitude of modern radio towers, passing messages at speeds unimaginable 150 years ago, and the heavy forest also shelters two dozen summer cabins and four campgrounds. The road is challengingly narrow, with some tight turns and great views, unobstructed by any guardrails, over the sheer slopes of the mountains.

As you enter the pines on your way up Forest Road 651, you pass the campground at Sulphide Del Rey. It's a pretty spot below the most nerve-racking parts of the road, but the campgrounds are more tent-friendly farther up the mountain. Continue to Pinal and Upper Pinal, nestled among white fir, ponderosa, and aspen near the top of the peaks. Upper Pinal, past the collection of summer cabins, consists of only three sites in a small cul-de-sac with a vault toilet, but two of the three are the shadiest, most private sites on the peak.

The sites, though unnumbered, are easily recognizable, with picnic tables, fire rings, and stonework done by the Civilian Conservation Corps (CCC). The first site on the loop is

Pinal Peak looks over the Dripping Spring Mountains to the south.

KEY INFORMATION

CONTACT: 928-402-6200, tinyurl.com
/upperpinal

OPEN: May–November

SITES: 3

EACH SITE HAS: Picnic table, fire ring;
some have an upright grill

ASSIGNMENT: First-come, first-served;
no reservations

REGISTRATION: Not required

AMENITIES: Vault toilets

PARKING: At campsites

FEE: None

ELEVATION: 7,500'

RESTRICTIONS:

PETS: On leash only

FIRES: In fire rings only

ALCOHOL: Permitted

VEHICLES: 16-foot length limit;
ATVs prohibited

QUIET HOURS: Not specified

OTHER: 14-day stay limit; bear-country
food-storage restrictions; pack in/pack
out; firearms prohibited; no drinking
water available

uphill among the trees, invisible from the road. You'll have room to park your vehicle below the campsite but not to turn around, so you will have to back in or back out. A CCC-built wall supports a leveled site with a picnic table, a fire ring with grill, and a flat, clear tent area. A trail behind you leads up toward Signal Peak and its fire tower. The table, fire ring, and upright grill at site 2 are right off of the turnaround, and the most tempting tent area is a marked flood zone, making this a better site for campers who sleep in their vehicle. Site 3, at the end of the cul-de-sac, also has a short, steep drive leading up to it. The nicely arranged site is defined by large boulders. You won't see your neighbors from any of the sites.

The campgrounds are never very crowded, but if Upper Pinal is full, you can return to Pinal and have your choice of 13 spots spread out on both sides of the road. The best sites are on the west side, on the hill at the north end of the campground. You're in alligator juniper and Gambel oak, and although your spot may have a little slope, the view from your tent across the valley below is spectacular.

You can choose among several hiking trails in these mountains, including the strenuous Sixshooter Trail 197 that leads from the Icehouse CCC picnic area to Upper Pinal Campground. This 6-mile one-way hike gains 3,000 feet in elevation and passes the remains of a former sawmill and an old mine entrance. (Rumor has it that Sixshooter was so named because the sawmill workers always seemed to be packing.) You can also make a loop hike by returning on the Telephone Trail 192, which runs along an underground telephone line and provides spectacular views of Globe and Miami below. In October the mountaintop blazes as the Gambel oak, aspens, maples, velvet ash, and Arizona walnut trees change color.

Pinal Peak is known as a prolific bird-watching area, a moist sky island on the north–south divide that attracts numerous migrant species. Several lightning-caused fires have damaged the habitat and discouraged the bird-watchers, and the slow process of recovery has been hampered by a major fire again in 2017, but the high-elevation climate keeps the birds coming back. Bring your telescope as well as your spotting scope since the stars are magnificent in the dark night. Black bears and mountain lions roam here, as do whitetail and mule deer. Leave the dog dish out and you may come face-to-face with a nosy skunk (we did).

On the other side of the mountain is Pioneer Pass Campground. This is a lovely canyon area, with several sites tucked behind boulders and invisible from the road. It was also developed by the CCC, and several of the original fieldstone tables and hearths can still be seen. The Kellner picnic site, which is available for large groups, is the only facility in the Pinal Mountain Recreation Area that charges a fee. Because of the lower elevation, you won't find pines, but a small stream running through the area provides sustenance for sycamores and oaks.

If you want to venture out of the campground, Globe's historic downtown displays a lot of interesting architecture from the early 1900s, and you'll find some neat antiques shops as well as many reminders of the region's ongoing mining heritage. Be sure to stop at the Besh-Ba-Gowah Archaeological Park to stand on the plaza of a partially restored 700-year-old Salado Indian pueblo and explore the small but very informative museum.

Upper Pinal Campground

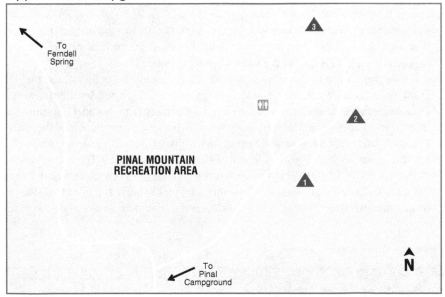

GETTING THERE

From Globe, follow signs for Pinal Mountain Recreation Area and Besh-Ba-Gowah Archaeological Park. Exit US 60 at Hill Street and go southeast 0.2 mile to Broad Street. Turn right and drive 300 feet west to Railroad Court/Jesse Hayes Road. Turn left, cross the railroad tracks, and take Jesse Hayes Road southeast 0.9 mile to Icehouse Canyon Road (FR 112). Turn right and head southwest 1.8 miles to FR 55. Turn right and drive southwest 2.5 miles to FR 651. Turn left and continue 10 miles to the Pinal Mountain Recreation Area. Continue 1 mile up the mountain to Upper Pinal.

GPS COORDINATES N33° 17.067' W110° 49.278'

25

⚠ Yavapai Campground

Beauty ★★★★ Privacy ★★★★ Spaciousness ★★★ Quiet ★★★ Security ★★★★ Cleanliness ★★★★★

The craggy peaks of Granite Mountain rise nearby.

Prescott began life when Arizona's first territorial governor set up the seat of government near the protection of Fort Whipple. It lost, regained, and lost again the title of territorial capital. Today it's one of the state's fastest-growing communities, with more people every year discovering the ideal Arizona climate in this mile-high city surrounded by lakes, mountains, and pine forests. Roll into town and you'll probably find an art fair or other event going on in the grassy square of the historic Yavapai County Courthouse in the center of downtown. Montezuma Street no longer has 40 saloons as it did in the good ol' days, but several bars keep historic Whiskey Row alive with nightly live music and dancing. The world's oldest continuously operating rodeo is held in Prescott, and the broncos buck and the cowboys strut annually during the week of Independence Day.

Just 8 miles northwest of downtown, Yavapai Campground butts up against the 9,799-acre Granite Mountain Wilderness, and the craggy peaks of Granite Mountain nearby rise to 7,626 feet. Twenty-one sites are arranged in a loop among large boulders (granite, naturally), scrub oak, cliff rose, manzanita, junipers, and ponderosa pines. All of the sites are well separated from one another and screened by chaparral, and each one has a picnic table and metal fire ring with grill. A few also have an upright grill. The two wheelchair-accessible sites, 6 and 17, are the only ones with electrical hookups. Sites 6 and 7 share a parking tab. Sites 11, 12, and 18 are our favorites. The picnic table and fire pit at site 11 are slightly separated from the parking area in a split-level design. Site 12 is set back so that you

A granite spire is your campsite sentinel.

KEY INFORMATION

CONTACT: 928-443-8000, tinyurl.com /yavapai-campground-az; reservations: 877-444-6777, recreation.gov

OPEN: Year-round when roads are open

SITES: 21

EACH SITE HAS: Picnic table, fire ring; some have an upright grill

ASSIGNMENT: By reservation; 3 sites are first-come, first-served

REGISTRATION: Self-register on-site

AMENITIES: Composting toilets, water spigots, boat ramp at Granite Basin Lake, beach, picnic area, picnic shelters, day-use area with ramadas, nature trails, group sites, campground host, wheelchair-accessible sites

PARKING: At campsites

FEE: $18/night single, $36/night double, $5/ additional vehicle; $10 online-reservation fee; $5 day use

ELEVATION: 5,600'

RESTRICTIONS:

PETS: On leash only, not permitted in lake

FIRES: In fire rings only

ALCOHOL: Permitted

VEHICLES: 40-foot length limit; 2 vehicles/site; 1 RV/site

QUIET HOURS: 10 p.m.–6 a.m.

OTHER: 14-day stay limit; mountain bikes prohibited; firearms prohibited; swimming prohibited, 10-person limit/site; electric motors only are allowed on the lake; mechanized and motorized vehicles prohibited in wilderness; check-in 2 p.m.; checkout 1 p.m.

can't see the road or any other sites—just trees, brush, and sky. A nearby boulder makes a good perch for watching the light change on Granite Mountain. Site 18 wins the award for the cutest site, with six steps leading up to the raised tent pad hidden behind a tall, slender granite monolith.

Just down the road is 5-acre Granite Basin Lake. The tiny lake is not stocked, but you can still throw out a line as an excuse just to sit a bit, and you might get a bite from a bluegill or catfish. Picnic tables and drinking water are available at the Playa Picnic Area. You'll usually find a selection of water birds here, including stately blue herons and contentious coots. The mountain looms across the lake, studded with enormous jagged outcrops of rock. Peregrine falcons and rock climbers are equally attracted to these rugged cliffs; if you're interested in climbing, check with the U.S. Forest Service about nesting closures and anchor rules.

Near the lake you'll also find Granite Group, a reservation-only area with varying fees for up to 100 people. While Yavapai Campground is open year-round, this group site is closed in the winter.

When you're ready to explore the network of trails around the campground, the host can provide you with a map of the Granite Basin Recreation Area. You can start your hike from the trailhead near site 11, or you can park at any of the four trailhead parking lots on the way down to the lake: Cayuse, Wekuvde, Metate, or at the boat launch. Granite Mountain Trail 261 begins at the Metate Trailhead and switchbacks up through the Granite Mountain Wilderness to Vista Point Overlook at one of the peaks. From here you can look out over the lake, Chino Valley, Skull Valley, and Prescott itself. The viewpoint is a strenuous 7.7-mile round-trip, but there's plenty of great stuff to see no matter how far you choose to go. Loop hikes of almost any length and difficulty can be designed by linking different trails in the Granite Basin Recreation Area. You'll also find connections to additional trails for hikers, equestrians, and mountain bikers that travel throughout the Prescott area, so stock up on topo maps.

If you've brought a canoe or kayak, Granite Lake won't hold your attention long. Venture over to nearby Watson Lake in the Granite Dells area of Prescott Valley. The weird formations of piled and tumbled billion-year-old boulders that surround the lower end of the lake are a paddler's playground, and there's terrific bird-watching in the marshy shallows where Granite Creek flows in. For a varied but easy hike, try the Peavine Trail, which follows a 4.75-mile section of the old Santa Fe, Prescott and Phoenix railroad grade from the Dells out into open rangeland.

Yavapai Campground

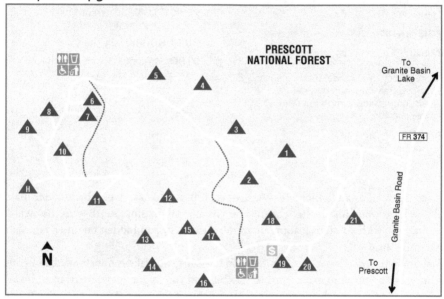

GETTING THERE

From Prescott, take Gurley Street west to Grove Avenue. Turn right and drive north 1 mile to Iron Springs Road. Turn left and continue northwest 3 miles to FR 374/Granite Basin Road. Turn right and then head north 3 miles to the campground entrance. Turn left into the campground.

GPS COORDINATES N34° 36.147' W112° 32.323'

MOGOLLON RIM

Fool Hollow (see campground 27, page 95) is a civilized lake with plenty of natural charm.

26

Chevelon Crossing Campground

Beauty ★★★★ Privacy ★★★ Spaciousness ★★ Quiet ★★★ Security ★★ Cleanliness ★★★

Only a mile upstream, large, cool swimming holes await.

The Mogollon Rim area is known for its tall pines and crystalline, trout-stocked lakes. The General Crook National Recreation Trail and its parallel route, Forest Road 300 or the Rim Road, wend their way along the 2,000-foot escarpment from east to west. The majority of rim-country traffic stays within a few miles of this road and the well-known lakes. North of the Mogollon Rim on FR 504 is Chevelon Crossing Campground, one of the smallest and least-used of the rim campgrounds. With only six sites on sloping, rocky ground in a canyon, this campground might seem an unlikely candidate for a best rating, but it's got a few outstanding features. Not the least of these is relatively light use at even the most popular times of year.

Chevelon Crossing is approachable from the south on either FR 504 or FR 169, which intersect near the bridge over Chevelon Creek. As you climb away from the rim, tall ponderosas fade into juniper and creosote, and you may wonder where you're headed, but in the canyon you find the pines again. Because the elevation is lower here than in the majority of the rim country, expect shrubbier trees and warmer summer temperatures. The campground, originally built by the Civilian Conservation Corps in the 1930s, is set on the slope of Chevelon Canyon overlooking the creek. Both are named for a trapper who died in the canyon after eating the roots of the water hemlock plant, a poisonous relative of the carrot.

Water persists along Chevelon Canyon even when the stream isn't flowing.

KEY INFORMATION

CONTACT: 928-535-4481, tinyurl.com
/cheveloncrossingcampground

OPEN: Year-round

SITES: 6

EACH SITE HAS: Picnic table, fire ring

ASSIGNMENT: First-come, first-served;
no reservations

REGISTRATION: Not required

AMENITIES: Vault toilets

PARKING: At campsites

FEE: None

ELEVATION: 6,300'

RESTRICTIONS:

PETS: On leash only

FIRES: In fire rings only

ALCOHOL: Permitted

VEHICLES: 16-foot length limit

QUIET HOURS: Not specified

OTHER: 14-day stay limit; pack in/pack out;
no drinking water available

Steep, rock walls rise across from the campground, forming a backdrop for the trees. The rocky, nominally perennial stream gets patchy in dry seasons (in fact, before Chevelon had his fatal dinner, it was called Big Dry Wash), but after heavy rains large, cool swimming holes await only a mile upstream.

The campsites are best suited for smaller tents and self-sufficient campers. Each site has a good, steel picnic table and fire ring (be sure to check fire restrictions on the information board) and some privacy from the other sites. Each site also has at least a two-person tentable area, but they're not purpose-made tent pads and may be a little sloped or rocky. There are vault toilets, but no water and no garbage service. The six unnumbered sites are arranged on the hillside in tiers, all with views across the canyon. The first three sites you come to are lined up along the creek side of the campground slightly below the road. Softer, shadier tent spots await below these sites near the creek. The third site may be the pick of the litter, with its own parking loop, shade from a big pine tree, and close proximity to the main trail that leads down to the creek. The remaining three sites are up the slope, nestled among the junipers. The fifth is nicely screened but very close to the road with no large tent spots.

While you're at Chevelon Crossing, take time to hike along Chevelon Creek. If you're self-contained and willing to haul your gear a little way, you'll find more camping options in a meadow just a short hike up the creek (south). Be aware of your impact here and properly dispose of your solid waste. The canyon is known for a healthy population of rattlesnakes and fire ants, so keep your eyes open as you're setting up camp. The trail runs from the meadow all the way to Chevelon Lake Dam. After 2 miles the trail becomes challenging and unmaintained, but in that short distance you can find some great swimming holes and spot wildlife, including beavers, skunks, mule deer, and plenty of birds.

You can fish for brown and rainbow trout in the pools of Chevelon Creek, but if you've come to the rim for fishing, you may want to try Chevelon Lake, 11 miles south of Chevelon Crossing off of FR 169 and 169B. Chevelon Lake, with its 200 acres of surface area, is the least accessible, most remote lake on the rim. Near the lake is a six-site campground with vault toilets that sees a bit more use than Chevelon Crossing. On maps, FR 169B appears to continue to the lake, but in reality it becomes an extremely rocky four-wheel-drive road and is closed to anything larger than an ATV just 0.25 mile past the campground. Boats with electric or 8-horsepower gas motors or less are allowed on the lake but have to be trekked down and back up the steep, 0.75-mile road (and boats left at the lake more than 24 hours may be confiscated!), so float tubes are more popular. The difficult access is to the trouts' benefit, and you may land a prizewinner here.

The trailhead sign you see in the Chevelon Crossing parking lot is not for a hiking trail, but rather for the north end of the Long Draw OHV Loop Trail, which encompasses 30 miles of forest roads; the south trailhead is located at Chevelon Lake Campground. At either campground you may encounter ATV and dirt-bike enthusiasts, and we've seen unmistakable evidence of equestrian occupation as well, but the area is usually so quiet that it's well worth taking a chance.

Chevelon Crossing Campground

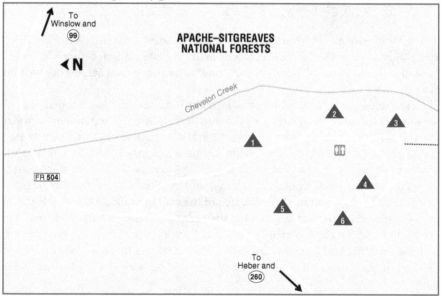

GETTING THERE

From Heber, take AZ 260 west 1 mile to FR 504. Turn right and drive north 18 miles to the campground.

From Winslow, take AZ 99 south 27 miles to FR 504. Turn left and travel southeast 7 miles to the campground.

GPS COORDINATES N34° 35.540' W110° 47.302'

27

Fool Hollow Lake Recreation Area Campground

Beauty ★★★ Privacy ★★ Spaciousness ★★ Quiet ★★★ Security ★★★★ Cleanliness ★★★★★

Fool Hollow offers lakeshore vistas from all campsites.

Remember what camping was like when you were a kid? Remember exploring all of the nature trails and paths that led into the woods, knowing the whole campground was yours to discover? Remember catching that sunfish that was so big that Dad had to help you reel it in? How about the hours spent playing card games in the tent, desperate for the rain to end? Being too impatient to hold your marshmallow over the hot coals and instead burning it in the direct flame? Fool Hollow Lake Recreation Area is the kind of campground where those childhood memories are made.

Lying within the city limits of Show Low, this campground is a perfect getaway for a family vacation. The area shares the tall pines and fine climate of the White Mountain Apache Reservation just to the south, but it hasn't always been a desirable location. When Thomas Westly Adair first settled here to farm in the 1880s, the locals joked that only a fool would try it. Although the town that bore Adair's name was swallowed by the lake in 1956, the area remains Fool Hollow. Opened in 1994, the park is a joint venture between Arizona

The sky shows off over peaceful waters.

KEY INFORMATION

CONTACT: 928-537-3680, 877-697-2757, azstateparks.com/fool-hollow

OPEN: Year-round

SITES: 31

EACH SITE HAS: Picnic table, fire ring, upright grill

ASSIGNMENT: By reservation

REGISTRATION: Purchase daily and annual passes at the park office

AMENITIES: Flush toilets, showers, amphitheater, boat ramp, water spigots, day-use ramadas, campground host, dump station, fish-cleaning stations, fishing docks, playground, firewood, ice, recycling, wheelchair-accessible sites

PARKING: At campsites

FEE: $20, $15/additional vehicle; $5 online-reservation fee

ELEVATION: 6,300'

RESTRICTIONS:

PETS: On leash only

FIRES: In fire rings only

ALCOHOL: Permitted

VEHICLES: 45-foot length limit

QUIET HOURS: 8 p.m.–7 a.m.

OTHER: Entrance gates closed 10 p.m.– 5 a.m.; 14-day stay limit; 10-horsepower boat-motor limit; no glass containers

State Parks, Apache–Sitgreaves National Forests, Arizona Game and Fish, the City of Show Low, and several corporate sponsors. The result of this collaboration is a well-managed and well-maintained park, nicely designed with smooth, accessible trails and modern facilities, as well as fishing and boating on the 150-acre lake.

Thirty-one of the sites at Fool Hollow lie on three paved loops named after locally seen raptors: Bald Eagle, Osprey, and Northern Harrier. Each of these no-hookup sites has its back to the east leg of the lake, providing lakeshore views for all. One official trail and any number of easy scrambles lead down the rocky slopes to the water's edge. The sites are in a ponderosa, pinyon, and juniper belt, and most have a reasonable amount of shade. While generally compact and quite close together, most of the sites offer enough level space to set up a couple of tents. About half of them share a paved parking tab, so you may find yourself in conversation with your neighbors. At 17 and 18 on the Osprey Loop, you'll find true double sites. Site 16 on the Osprey Loop and site 25 on Bald Eagle are designed to be wheelchair-accessible, as are the shower and toilet facilities. Sites 15, 16, 20, 24, and 31 provide a little more distance from nearby campers.

Each site contains a picnic table, steel fire ring, and upright grill, as well as a cleared tent area. Only sites 29, 30, and 31 are within sight and (possibly) hearing of the campground's RV-friendly section. The sites usually fill up during the summer peak, but reservations can be made online. A resident campground host can be found just down the road in the RV section on Mallard Loop, where you can also buy firewood and ice. The park is open year-round, but come prepared for cold nights (and possibly snow) October–April, and for the usual summer afternoon rains.

The day-use area offers playgrounds, a separate boat ramp, and group ramadas that are available by reservation and can accommodate up to 200 people. They are a popular choice for both local citizens and tourists for family reunions and birthday parties. These facilities sit across the lake from the campground, reducing traffic through the sites. Another playground across from the Osprey Loop provides a safe, enjoyable place close to your site for the kids to meet new friends.

Fool Hollow is one of the friendliest campgrounds we've seen for people with limited mobility—even the fishing docks down by the boat ramp are wheelchair-accessible. Fishing is the main attraction here, with a large variety of species (including rainbow and brown trout, bass, northern pike, crappies, and catfish) waiting to be lured from the depths of the lake. Regulations allow boats with motors up to 10 horsepower. Swimming is allowed but there is no designated swimming area, and no lifeguards or facilities are provided; stay close to your boat or the shore and watch out for stray fishhooks. The easy trail around the south end of the lake provides terrific bird-watching opportunities, particularly during migrations.

The town of Show Low supposedly got its name from a card game played by two ranchers for possession of the valley rangeland that would become one of Arizona's most pleasant summer havens. Legend says Marion Clark told Corydon Cooley, "Show low and you win," and Cooley cut the cards, coming up with the deuce of clubs (now a civic emblem). Gas, groceries, restaurants, and shops can be found within minutes of the recreation area, and park rangers will give you information on the White Mountains Trail System and other local attractions.

Fool Hollow Lake Recreation Area Campground

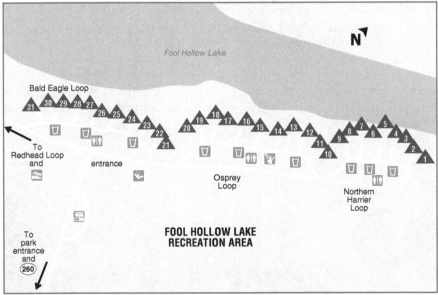

GETTING THERE

From Show Low, take AZ 260 west 2 miles to Old Linden Road. Turn right and then drive 0.6 mile to Fool Hollow Lake Road.

GPS COORDINATES N34° 16.450' W110° 03.898'

28

⛺ FR 9350 Dispersed Camping Area

Beauty ★★★★★ Privacy ★★★★ Spaciousness ★★★★ Quiet ★★★ Security ★★★ Cleanliness ★★★

Half of the sites perch at the edge of the 2,000-foot escarpment.

Just 90 miles north of Phoenix, after a beautiful drive along the Beeline Highway 87 through the Mazatzal Mountains, you arrive in the old mining and lumber town of Payson. The saguaros have disappeared, replaced by pine trees; the temperature decreases as your elevation increases. This is rim country. The town sits at the base of the Mogollon Rim, pronounced *muggy-own* and named after Spanish governor Juan Ignacio Flores Mogollon. In town, turn right at the stoplight and take AZ 260 east, with the rim looming above you to the north and the Hellsgate Wilderness spreading out below to the south.

Stop at the visitor center, on the right as you finally top the rim, and talk to the U.S. Forest Service rangers and volunteers about the area. On one July afternoon, caught inside during a downpour, we chatted with ranger Paul Schilke, who told us about several designated dispersed camping areas on the Mogollon Rim. Ranger Schilke said the best camping on the rim is on Forest Road 9350, and we agree. Half the dispersed sites along this road actually perch at the edge of the 2,000-foot escarpment, with 180° views across miles of mountains and valleys below. In our opinion, the view is second only to the Grand Canyon, and on top of it all, it's free.

To get there, turn off AZ 260 opposite the visitor center, onto the Rim Road (FR 300), passing the turnoff for popular Woods Canyon Lake. On your way, stop at any of the three scenic overlooks to see what's in store for you. Continue 2 miles past where the pavement ends and turn left on FR 9350.

Sleep tight at the very edge of the Colorado Plateau.

KEY INFORMATION

CONTACT: 928-535-4481, tinyurl.com/fr9350

OPEN: Year-round when roads are open

SITES: 42

EACH SITE HAS: Fire ring, some have a picnic table

ASSIGNMENT: First-come, first-served; no reservations

REGISTRATION: Not required

AMENITIES: Vault toilet at trailhead; campground host

PARKING: At campsites

FEE: None

ELEVATION: 7,600'

RESTRICTIONS:

PETS: On leash only

FIRES: In fire rings only

ALCOHOL: Permitted

VEHICLES: No restrictions; high clearance recommended for some sites

QUIET HOURS: Not specified

OTHER: 14-day stay limit; pack in/pack out; bear-country food-storage restrictions; firearms prohibited; firewood gathering prohibited; 10-person limit/site; not recommended for families with young children or anyone with a fear of heights

The campsites scatter 1.25 miles along both sides of FR 9350, but you'll find the coveted rim sites to the south. If possible, grab 7, 21, 22, 24, or 26; from these sites you have your own private scenic overlook and can see the rim drop nearly straight down below you (this recommendation may not suit families with small children or those with a fear of heights). There, the same tall ponderosa pines that tower over you in camp look like bonsai trees and soon meld into a green, rolling carpet spreading as far as the eye can see.

A few of the rim sites where the road runs closer to the edge are shallow and compact. But if you're willing to sacrifice some view to gain a bit of space, the sites on the north side tend to be large enough for multiple tents and vehicles, and are tucked well back—100 feet or more—from the road. Site 31 sits almost 400 feet back in the trees, but you'll find the best combination of solitude and stunning views at site 36.

After site 38, the road curves away from the rim and the ponderosas make way for oaks and a small clearing. The road is closed at the end of FR 9350, so all traffic must double back, and the last few sites away from the rim will see the fewest passersby. A numbered fiberglass post at the road marks each site, and another within the site indicates roughly where you should camp. You'll find a stone fire ring and usually a picnic table but no trash service. The only restroom is at the Carr Lake Trailhead, near the entrance. If you get to the end and find the campground full, which commonly occurs on summer weekends, check out nearby dispersed areas at FR 9354. Although these sites lack the rim views of FR 9350, they are still beautiful, wooded, private sites.

Be sure to bring your jacket; even during tank-top-and-flip-flop weather in Phoenix, the air is much cooler here at 7,600 feet. The pines, aspens, and oaks shade you during the heat of the day and make hiking pleasurable. Be wary during summer thunderstorms—the rim is said to have one of the country's highest frequencies of lightning strikes.

The Drew Canyon Trail 291 works its way through the campground and drops 800 feet in 1 mile to connect with the Highline National Recreation Trail. The Highline Trail 31, first blazed in the late 1880s, runs 51 miles along the base of the rim. Today it serves as the central hub for an extensive network of trails above and below the escarpment, some of which comprise a portion of the Arizona Trail. Part of the network of trails that traverses the entire state from Mexico to Utah, this section begins near Pine, traveling with the Highline Trail to the East Verde River and up and over the rim to FR 300. Above the rim, the General George Crook National Recreation Trail travels for more than 100 miles, tracing the route that its famous namesake established as a supply line from Camp Verde to Fort Apache during the Apache Wars. Along the rim it parallels FR 300, but hikers, bikers, and equestrians can follow the chevrons, and even some of the frontier army's remaining blazes, along the original track.

There's a lot more to do and see in the rim country, also well known for its many lakes and streams. For more details, see the Chevelon Crossing and Knoll Lake profiles (pages 92 and 104, respectively).

FR 9350 Dispersed Camping Area

GETTING THERE

From Payson, take AZ 260 east 35 miles to FR 300. Turn left and drive north 5.25 miles to FR 9350. Turn left to enter the campground.

GPS COORDINATES N34° 20.253' W110° 58.273'

29

Haigler Canyon Campground

Beauty ★★★★ Privacy ★★★ Spaciousness ★★★ Quiet ★★★ Security ★★★★ Cleanliness ★★★★

The Sierra Anchas are some of the most beautiful yet least-traveled mountains in central Arizona.

Haigler Canyon Campground sits along perennial Haigler Creek, just north of the small ranching town of Young and beneath the Mogollon Rim, the 2,000-foot escarpment that separates the Colorado Plateau from the lower valleys and deserts. The creek is fed by natural springs and stocked with brown and rainbow trout through the spring and summer. Sycamores, cottonwoods, and Gambel oaks burst into a flurry of color during the fall and early winter.

This campground received a major makeover in 2007. Previously, dispersed camping sites were arranged along the banks of the creek. The renovation resulted in two camping areas outside of the flood channel, significantly reducing human impact on the creek and surrounding vegetation. Near the water crossing, seven sites back the creekbed. The parallel, level parking tabs are evenly spaced 100 feet apart, with oaks, junipers, and a few ponderosa pines growing between. These spots have obviously been created with RVs or trailers in mind, although there's room to set up a tent near the picnic tables. If you want to be as close to the creek as possible, try for site 2 or 3, both of which are a little shadier than the others. You should know, though, that better tent sites wait just up the road.

The Sonoran Desert stretches away to the west.

KEY INFORMATION

CONTACT: 928-462-4300, tinyurl.com /haiglercanyon

OPEN: Full services April–November

SITES: 14 (7 walk-in tent sites)

EACH SITE HAS: Picnic table, fire ring

ASSIGNMENT: First-come, first-served; no reservations

REGISTRATION: Self-register on-site

AMENITIES: Vault toilets

PARKING: At campsites, group parking for walk-in sites

FEE: $8/night with Tonto Pass

ELEVATION: 5,300'

RESTRICTIONS:

PETS: On leash only

FIRES: In fire rings only

ALCOHOL: Permitted

VEHICLES: 16-foot length limit

QUIET HOURS: 10 p.m.–6 a.m.

OTHER: 14-day stay limit; bear-country food-storage restrictions

A second area on the opposite side of the road offers seven walk-in sites in the oaks and alligator junipers. Designed specifically for tenters, each has an assigned parking space with its own trail leading to the site. A few extra parking spots are provided, but primarily it's one vehicle per site. Site 8 is the only exception, with pull-in parking similar to the lower sites. All sites consist of level, graveled rectangles with plenty of space for a couple of tents, a fire pit with a grill, and a picnic table with a wheelchair-accessible overhang on one side. Manzanita and shrub oaks between the sites give them some privacy. Forest Road 200 circles the campground, coming a little close to sites 8, 9, and 14, but the road rarely receives enough use for traffic noise or dust to be much of an issue. Site 9 sits farther back than 8 and feels nicely secluded despite the road. All of the sites should have some afternoon shade, but 12 and 13 promise cool mornings and evenings; these are our favorite picks. An additional site at the tent loop's entrance is intended for a host, but as of press time the campground is not hosted.

It's a short walk to the creek from the tent sites, but you'll find two nice picnic areas with restrooms much closer to the water. There are a number of more-or-less developed trails along the creek to enjoy. If you forgot to purchase your Tonto Pass ahead of time, free campsites are available at nearby Alderwood Campground, also situated along Haigler Creek.

Just a mile up FR 200 is the trailhead for the Bear Flat Trail 178, an old jeep trail that leads into the Hellsgate Wilderness. Hellsgate encompasses 37,440 acres of rugged mountains and steep canyons carved by Haigler and Tonto Creeks; at their confluence in a deep gorge is Hell's Gate. The best way to access Hell's Gate is by the Hell's Gate Trail 37. You'll find the trailhead off of FR 405, near Little Green Valley and Ponderosa Campground. Note that the best access is rated at most difficult and requires 11 miles of steep climbs and downhill scrambles before reaching the final descent to the water—this wilderness is truly wild and only for the fit and adventurous. As always, motorized and mechanized vehicles are forbidden in the wilderness.

You are more than a mile high here and can expect four distinct seasons. The best time to visit is in the spring when the creek will be flowing strongly, or in the fall when you can catch the leaves changing in the Sierra Ancha Mountains. As you drive from the campground to Young, you'll pass by the gravesite of the unnamed Navajo sheepherder who was the first victim of the long-lasting Pleasant Valley War, an infamous feud between the Tewksbury and Graham clans. In Young, long tamed but still a ranching town, you will find two restaurants, a grocery store, a gas station, and lodging. You can reach Haigler Creek easily by coming south from AZ 260, although in places the road becomes one lane, hugging tight around blind curves with sheer drops (your passengers will enjoy the view). To enjoy the full beauty of this area, drive the length of AZ 288 from Roosevelt Lake to the rim or vice versa. The Sierra Anchas are some of the most beautiful yet least-traveled mountains in central Arizona.

Haigler Canyon Campground

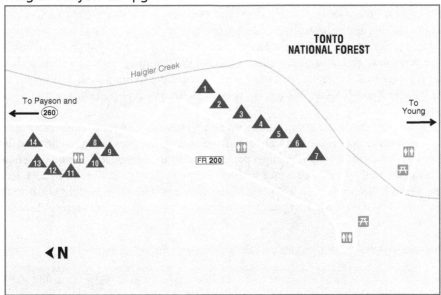

GETTING THERE

From Young, take FR 512 north 3 miles to FR 200. Turn left and drive 9 miles to the campground.

From Payson, take AZ 260 east 24 miles to FR 291. Turn right and drive southeast for 3 miles to FR 200. Turn right and continue southeast 5 miles to the campground.

GPS COORDINATES N34° 13.262' W110° 57.803'

30

⛺ Knoll Lake Campground

Beauty ★★★ Privacy ★★★ Spaciousness ★★★★ Quiet ★★★ Security ★★★ Cleanliness ★★★★★

Cast a line from the rocky shoreline or bring a small boat.

The Mogollon Rim is a sheer palisade of limestone and sandstone cliffs that runs diagonally across much of Arizona, marking the boundary between the Sonoran Desert lowlands and the Colorado Plateau. As you climb northward from the Valley of the Sun, you leave behind the realm of ocotillo and saguaro for a dense forest of ponderosa pine. The dramatic, canyon-carved slopes rise to more than 7,000 feet, and among the trees are scattered springs, streams, and a dozen lakes, making this one of the state's most popular summer destinations. Split between two national forests, Coconino in the west and Apache–Sitgreaves in the east, the rim country offers a plethora of camping, from primitive, secluded, dispersed sites to RV-friendly recreation areas. Knoll Lake Campground, just up the road from 75-acre Knoll Lake, strikes a good balance, with 33 developed sites nestled among the trees.

The campground is laid out in an uneven figure eight, with the site numbers increasing as you go counterclockwise. It's nicely organized so that the sites near the entrance (sites 2–6 and 33) have pull-throughs or larger parking tabs to accommodate RVs and trailers, and the rest of the well-spaced sites better suit tent campers. Major renovations in 2006 left all campsites with cleared, leveled tent pads, nice concrete picnic tables, upright grills, and fire rings. Several sites offer two tent pads and two picnic tables. The larger loop circles a small

Thick evergreen forest makes hiking a pleasurable adventure on this part of the rim.

KEY INFORMATION

CONTACT: 928-477-2255, tinyurl.com
/knolllake

OPEN: Mid-May–October, depending
on weather

SITES: 33

EACH SITE HAS: Picnic tables, fire ring,
upright grills

ASSIGNMENT: First-come, first-served;
no reservations

REGISTRATION: With camp host

AMENITIES: Vault toilets, boat ramp,
water spigots

PARKING: At campsites

FEE: $14/night single, $28/night double

ELEVATION: 7,400'

RESTRICTIONS:

PETS: On leash only

FIRES: In fire rings only

ALCOHOL: Permitted

VEHICLES: 32-foot length limit;
ATVs prohibited

QUIET HOURS: 10 p.m.–6 a.m.

OTHER: 14-day stay limit; horses prohibited;
off-road vehicles prohibited except to enter
and exit campground; 1-horsepower
electric boat-motor limit; discharging of
firearms prohibited; checkout 1 p.m.;
8-person limit/site, 2 vehicles/site

hill, so sites inside the loop are up on the hillside and sites outside the loop are set below or away from the road. Sites 20 (a double) and 18 are well below the road, with stone stairs leading down to them. These sites feel much more secluded and private. Sites 23–25 are on the edge of their own loop and spacious enough for larger groups.

Knoll Lake Campground fills up during the summer season and occasionally gets folks who've come to party by firelight, but for the most part the campers are families up to enjoy the cool water and great scenery. Knoll Lake is neither as primitive as nearby Bear Canyon nor as bustling as its larger neighbor, the Aspen Campground at Woods Canyon Lake. On weekends the woods are full of dispersed campers as well. The meadowlarks are louder, but you may hear engine noise or the occasional whoop and holler.

The high elevation means cool, comfortable temperatures during summer, but expect heavy rains (even hail!) from July to September during the monsoon season. While driving, keep an eye out for deer and especially elk, which are large enough to completely cover the windshield of your average sedan (don't ask us how we know). The Arizona Game and Fish Department, Arizona Department of Transportation, Federal Highway Administration, and the U.S. Forest Service developed the world's first elk crosswalk along AZ 260, where the elk are funneled either under or across the road. Where underpasses are impractical, flashing signs notify motorists when nearby animals trigger the electronic sensors.

Just a mile down the road from the campground is Knoll Lake, named for the former hilltop that now forms a small island in its center. Brook, brown, and rainbow trout are stocked here. Cast a line from the rocky shoreline or bring a small boat. The lake is restricted to electric motors only and is favored by people with kayaks, canoes, or kickboats.

Hiking, biking, and riding trails crisscross the area, including the strenuous 5.3-mile Babe Haught Trail which leaves Knoll Lake and heads down off the Mogollon Rim following an old pioneer supplies trail. Nearby Barbershop Trail, U-Bar Trail, Houston Brothers Trail, and Fred Haught Trail make up the Cabin Loop Trail System that visits several early 1900s U.S. Forest Service fire guard cabins, including one that Gifford Pinchot, first chief of the USFS, deemed the most picturesque. The Blue Ridge passage of the Arizona Trail passes through this area from Forest Road 300 to AZ 87. The 100-mile General Crook Trail runs relatively flat along the Mogollon Rim, with spectacular views over Payson and the Hellsgate Wilderness to the Mazatzal and Sierra Ancha Mountains. The trail parallels FR 300, a graded gravel route also known as the Rim Road, which can be combined with FR 321, FR 96, FR 95, and AZ 87 to make a 60-mile scenic drive looping through the rim country. This is an especially good trip to take in the fall when the leaves are changing. Pine and Strawberry, along AZ 87, offer gas, groceries, lodging, and special events throughout the year, and in August Payson boasts what it claims is the world's oldest continuous rodeo. For another superlative, see the world's largest travertine natural bridge at Tonto Natural Bridge State Park, just south of Pine.

Knoll Lake Campground

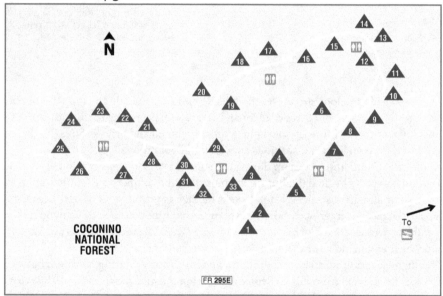

GETTING THERE

From Payson, take AZ 260 east 29 miles to the Rim Road (FR 300). Turn left and continue northwest 21 miles to FR 295E. Turn right and drive north 3.5 miles to the campground.

GPS COORDINATES N34° 25.547' W111° 05.642'

31

Rose Creek Campground

Beauty ★★★★ Privacy ★★★ Spaciousness ★★★★ Quiet ★★★★ Security ★★★ Cleanliness ★★★

The road passes many deep side canyons full of sharp pinnacles and hoodoos, then suddenly plunges into sun-dappled forest.

The trip from Globe to Young along the Desert to Tall Pines Scenic Drive (AZ 288) takes you from the sere valley around Roosevelt Lake to the ponderosa pines, maples, and aspens blanketing the Sierra Ancha Mountains. Rounding the southern end of the lake, you cross the Salt River near the Roosevelt Lake Diversion Dam, the end of a day's trip for many rafters on the upper Salt. As you climb higher you see down the length of 22,000-acre Roosevelt Lake, which looks even larger in its mountainous setting. The road passes many deep side canyons full of sharp pinnacles and hoodoos, then suddenly plunges into sun-dappled forest. From this point, pavement alternates with smooth gravel.

You soon reach Sawmill Flats, the first of several camping opportunities on the way to Young. The history is reflected in the name, but all that remains now are the "flats" that form this small, dispersed area among tall, second-growth ponderosas. Continue a few miles on to reach Rose Creek Campground, six pleasant sites lining an intermittent creek that you

In season, wild-grape vines climb the trees at Rose Creek.

KEY INFORMATION

CONTACT: 928-462-4300, tinyurl.com
/rosecreekcampground

OPEN: April–November

SITES: 5

EACH SITE HAS: Fire pit, picnic
table, grill

ASSIGNMENT: First-come, first-served;
no reservations

REGISTRATION: Not required

AMENITIES: Vault toilet

PARKING: At campsites

FEE: None

ELEVATION: 6,100'

RESTRICTIONS:

PETS: On leash only

FIRES: In fire rings only

ALCOHOL: Permitted

VEHICLES: 16-foot length limit;
ATVs prohibited

QUIET HOURS: Not specified

OTHER: 14-day stay limit; bear-country food-
storage requirements; pack in/pack out

will ford to get to the campground. Rose Creek is small and feels a bit forgotten, but you are likely to have the place all to yourself. Sycamores, maples, and Gambel oaks paint the canyon in the late fall or early winter. The raspberry bushes and wild grape vines create a lush understory that screens the sites. Each site comes equipped with a fire pit, a picnic table with extra overhang for wheelchairs, and an upright grill. We especially liked the last, secluded site on the turnaround, site 6. Site 4 is the most open of the sites and might be best for a van or truck camper.

Once you're settled in, you can drive up to Workman Creek Recreation Area and hike or drive to where Workman Falls drops 200 sheer vertical feet. The falls were barely flowing when we visited in October, but during monsoons or snowmelt they've been described as "thundering." If you dare the drive farther up Forest Road 487, take advantage of the pull-over at the top, where you can walk down and peer (carefully) right over the edge.

Continue on (high-clearance vehicle recommended) and you'll pass trailheads for some of the Sierra Ancha Wilderness's many trails. Wildlife abounds, including elk, mule and whitetail deer, javelina, black bear, and mountain lion. People have also lived here from ages past, and the canyons are scattered with the ruins of generations of cliff dwellings.

The road eventually leads to the highest point in the Sierra Anchas, 7,694-foot Aztec Peak. The fire watchtower rises high above; from there, you can see all the way to Roosevelt Lake, the Four Peaks, and the Mogollon Rim. Nearby is a mysterious and painstakingly constructed stone living room, where you can sit in two primeval lounge chairs (complete with cup holders) that face a vast hearth with Arizona as a backdrop.

Heading back to AZ 288 and continuing north, you'll pass over the Honey Creek Divide—another dispersed camping area. Soon you'll see the broad, grassy valley that harbors Young, one of the few true cow towns left in Arizona. Historically, Young is best known for the Graham-Tewksbury Feud, one of the West's bloodiest and most iconic range wars. Also known as the Pleasant Valley War, it was the raw material for Zane Grey's novel *To the Last Man.* Today Young is still home to working ranches, although you'll see llamas as well as cows. You'll find two restaurants and one gas station in town. If you continue north from Young, AZ 288 becomes FR 512, a graded dirt road with panoramic vistas of the Tonto Basin, which climbs the Mogollon Rim and connects with AZ 260.

Although parts of AZ 288 are now paved, Young residents are divided about finishing the job; some hope for the development and prosperity that's come to towns like Payson, and others would like to preserve the quiet and traditions of this "high lonesome" country. Whichever way it goes, they'll settle it peaceably this time, but come yourself and enjoy the Sierra Anchas before the rest of the crowd discovers them.

Rose Creek Campground

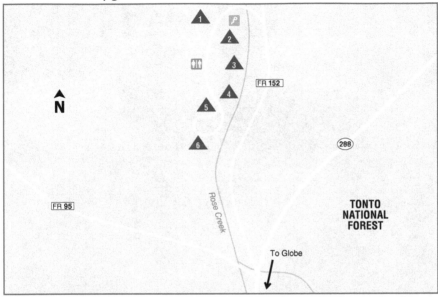

GETTING THERE

From Globe, take AZ 88 north 16 miles to AZ 288. Turn right and travel 23 miles to FR 152. Turn left to the campground.

GPS COORDINATES N33° 49.685′ W110° 58.746′

WHITE MOUNTAINS

The morning sun shines after a cool night at Buffalo Crossing Campground along East Fork (see campground 34, page 117).

Blue Crossing Campground

Beauty ★★★★ Privacy ★★★★★ Spaciousness ★★★ Quiet ★★★★ Security ★★★ Cleanliness ★★★

Intriguing red sandstone formations appear and disappear as the foliage around you grows more lush.

The Blue River is cool and clear, surrounded by lush greenery, steep canyon walls, tall ponderosa pines, and plenty of history. Driving south on the Blue River Road (Forest Road 281) from Alpine, you descend on dirt switchbacks, following the river over a series of one-lane bridges that gradually lengthen as the canyon grows deeper. Intriguing red sandstone formations appear and disappear as the foliage around you grows more lush. The tall pines linger, but the canyon floor becomes the domain of willows and wild grapes. The road is graded and quite smooth, with a few tight squeezes and curves. During rainy seasons, the road may be muddy, with rocks, branches, or other debris washed down from the upper slopes. Passenger cars should be fine except in very wet or icy conditions.

Some miles of the road make you feel as if you're really traveling into the wilderness, but suddenly a mailbox will appear incongruously by a dirt drive. As the canyon opens into a small, green valley, it's hard not to envy the people who have been lucky enough to live here. The Blue River once flowed through this community with enough force to float logs down to the mining town of Clifton, but the river has dwindled over the last century,

The Blue River can be heard chuckling from every site.

KEY INFORMATION

CONTACT: 928-339-5000, tinyurl.com
/bluecrossingcampground

OPEN: May–October

SITES: 4

EACH SITE HAS: Picnic table, fire ring, some
have an Adirondack shelter

ASSIGNMENT: First-come, first-served;
no reservations

REGISTRATION: Not required

AMENITIES: Vault toilets

PARKING: At campsites

FEE: None

ELEVATION: 5,800'

RESTRICTIONS:

PETS: On leash only

FIRES: In fire rings only

ALCOHOL: Permitted

VEHICLES: 16-foot length limit

QUIET HOURS: 10 p.m.–6 a.m.

OTHER: 14-day stay limit; pack in/pack
out; mountain bikes prohibited in the
Blue Range Primitive Area; bear-country
food-storage requirements; no drinking
water available

and since the U.S. Forest Service (USFS) began a concerted effort to reduce overgrazing, many of the ranches have gone out of business. Signs by the road, however, still invite you to help the Blue River Cowbelles, a local group of ranch women, to keep the valley clean, safe, and beautiful.

Blue, Arizona, now borders the Blue Range Primitive Area, 173,762 acres of wilderness accessible by hiking or horseback riding only. Contact the USFS for information on the area's many trails. The Blue River is no longer stocked, but you can find wild brown and rainbow trout during spring and fall. The endangered Mexican gray wolf has been reintroduced in the Blue Range area, and many other animals, especially elk, thrive here.

The Upper Blue Campground, 14 miles south of Alpine, consists of just three sites on a small loop among alligator junipers and Gambel oak. At two of the sites, the USFS has restored the log Adirondack shelters built by the Civilian Conservation Corps (CCC) during the Great Depression. This is a pleasant area, but you're a little separated from the river here. Past Upper Blue, the vegetation gets thicker and more lush. You pass through more private property, so don't look for dispersed camping along FR 281, and keep your eyes open for loose cattle. On your left shortly before you reach the intersection with FR 567 is the one-room Blue School.

Following the signs, take a right on FR 567 and ford the river. Note the depth marker and use good judgment trying to cross! The turnoff to Blue Crossing Campground is just past the ford on the right, and a short drive takes you back into a shady four-site loop. As at Upper Blue, you'll find no amenities beyond picnic tables, steel fire rings, vault toilets, and a couple of log lean-tos. The first site, while quite open to the road, has a nice arrangement of CCC shelter, table and fire pit, and a large, flat area under the trees. Site 2 is smaller and closer to the road with barely a pulloff for parking, but also has a shelter with a medium-sized tent area next to it. Site 3 has good parking, a large, shady tent area, and some screening, and you can clearly hear the stream just a short walk behind you. Site 4, at the end of the tiny parking loop, is shallow and open but has a couple of flat tent spots. Most of the time, you will be the only campers here; the busiest seasons are in spring or in fall when the campground is used by hunters.

Between sites 3 and 4 you can see the stone steps that were the original entrance, with one of several interpretive signs around the campground. On the other side of site 4 is a short trail that leads through a gate to a rocky outcropping with mysterious symbols pecked into the surface. The Mogollon people left these petroglyphs more than 700 years ago, and although their meaning is now lost, they still speak to us about the long history of habitation in this green valley.

An alternate route into Blue Crossing—FR 567, also known as Red Hill Road—climbs steeply out of the valley from the river to intersect US 191, just a few miles north of Hannagan Meadow. A beautiful drive with stunning views of the Blue Range Primitive Area, this route is not for the faint of heart or those with a short attention span. Drive carefully and avoid it in tricky weather. During wet seasons and particularly the spring snow melt, check with the USFS for conditions on the road and the river crossing. For more details on the Hannagan Meadow area, see profile 36, KP Cienega Campground (page 123).

Blue Crossing Campground

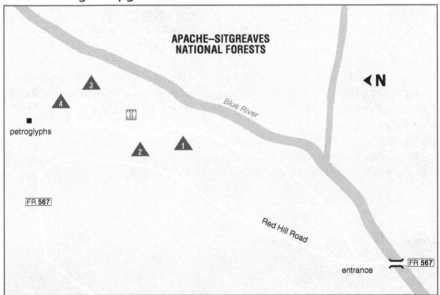

GETTING THERE

From Alpine, take US 180 east 4 miles to FR 281. Turn right and drive south 23 miles to FR 567. Turn right, cross the river, and turn right into the campground.

From Hannagan Meadow, take US 191 north 7 miles to FR 567. Turn right and travel southeast 13 miles to the campground.

GPS COORDINATES N33° 37.673' W109° 05.880'

33

Brookchar Campground

Beauty ★★★ Privacy ★★★ Spaciousness ★★★ Quiet ★★★ Security ★★★ Cleanliness ★★★

Roll down your car windows and enjoy the brisk summer air.

Rolling, grassy hills bordered by pines and a wide, blue sky welcome you as you drive windy AZ 261 on the way to Big Lake Recreation Area. The green is a welcome sight for dry eyes used to the desert dust and thirsting for moisture. This is roll-down-the-car-window country, so turn off the air conditioner and let the delightfully brisk summer air whip through your hair. High in the White Mountains in the Apache-Sitgreaves National Forests, 450-acre Big Lake and its smaller sibling, 100-acre Crescent Lake, await with tantalizing cool, blue water.

Big Lake may not be big by other states' standards, but for Arizona it is a respectable size. And besides, it's not the size of the lake that matters, it's the number of campgrounds you can fit around it. By those standards, Big Lake ranks near the top, competing with other biggies such as vast Roosevelt Lake. Big Lake boasts five campgrounds, each named after a trout species—the lake's main attraction. The campgrounds vary in amenities and style to appeal to everyone.

When you first arrive, stop at the visitor center if it's open (hours have varied in the past due to tight budgets) and see what public programs may be on offer. Whether the visitor center is open or closed, you can pick up the pamphlet for the 0.5-mile, self-guided trail that runs behind the center.

The next left will bring you to Rainbow, the suburban gated community of campgrounds. Here and at full-hookup Apache Trout, on the other end of the campground chain, are where most of the RVs hang out. If you prefer a tent spot without hookups, follow the contour of

Golden aspens ring site 12 on a fall evening.

KEY INFORMATION

CONTACT: 928-333-6200, tinyurl.com
/brookchar; reservations: 877-444-6777,
recreation.gov

OPEN: Year-round when roads are open;
full services mid-May–October

SITES: 13

EACH SITE HAS: Picnic table, fire ring

ASSIGNMENT: First-come, first-served or
by reservation

REGISTRATION: With camp host

AMENITIES: Vault toilets, campground host,
water spigots, tent cabin rental, boat
launch, boat rentals, general store, hot
showers, flush toilets, dump station nearby,
interpretive activities and programs

PARKING: Walk-in

FEE: $16/night; $10 online-reservation fee

ELEVATION: 9,000'

RESTRICTIONS:

PETS: On leash only

FIRES: In fire rings only

ALCOHOL: Permitted

VEHICLES: No RVs or trailers; 1 vehicle/site

QUIET HOURS: 10 p.m.–6 a.m.

OTHER: 14-day stay limit;
10-horsepower boat-motor limit;
bear-country food-storage requirements;
firearm use prohibited

the lake to Grayling Campground. Designed to appeal to either style of camping, the campground offers paved roads and sites with pull-throughs or large parking tabs, but they're spread well apart and there are some nice tent spots. At Grayling you get a shady site among the trees but no lake view.

We recommend staying at Brookchar, the campground designated for tent campers. Here you'll find 13 walk-in, tent-only, reservable sites on a hillside, and many have a great view of the lake. There is also a large cabin tent at site 7 available for rent if you don't want to bother with setting up your own tent or want some shelter from the monsoon storms. The host resides in site 1 from mid-May through October. Sites 2–6 are private sites set back in the woods behind the host site, although the flush toilets are part of your lake view. Sites 8 and 9 have little shade and are located a short distance from the parking lot. Site 10 and 11 are tucked back in the woods; walk through to get all the way back to site 13. Our favorite is site 12, which is screened by undergrowth from the rest of Brookchar and has its own parking tab directly across the road from the lake. Your tent is sheltered by aspens, yet you still have a great sunset view through the trees.

Once past the Brookchar parking lot, the next left up a dirt one-way loop takes you to Cutthroat, another favorite of ours. The road is narrow and the parking pullouts small, so you probably won't find even a pop-up trailer here. Most of the sites are walk-in sites on the inside of the loop, on a wooded hillside overlooking Big Lake. Site 3, which is nicely secluded, has its own parking off the road. Site 12 is large and well screened, with no close neighbors. The forest turns to meadow near sites 13–17, giving them an open feel and unobscured lake views. Sites 5, 6, 10, and 11 are the closest to the lake, with parking off the main road.

Expect heavy rains and lake-clearing lightning on afternoons in July–September. We've seen rainwater running in rivulets down through the campsites, so keep that in mind while choosing your site and setting up your gear. During the winter, the lake is open to ice fishing, but the roads may be impassable due to snow. Brave souls can reach the lake by snowmobile, and camping is free after mid-October. In season, Big Lake Tackle and Supply offers boat rentals, fishing licenses, souvenirs, groceries, gas, clothing, and tackle and bait.

If you've already caught your allotment of fish, the woods are riddled with trails to explore. Indian Springs Trail 627 starts from loop D of the Rainbow Campground and travels along an old railway line, making a 7.5-mile loop alternating between cool pine forests and wildflower-dappled meadows. A mile-long spur trail leads to the Big Lake fire lookout tower. The tower is usually staffed in the summer, so ask the lookout if you can climb up and enjoy the view. Another spur leads to the West Fork Trail 628, which eventually takes you along the West Fork of the Black River—one of the most beautiful areas in Arizona.

Nearby Mount Baldy rises to 11,403 feet, and hiking up East Baldy Trail 95 or West Baldy Trail 94 provides unparalleled vistas. The East Baldy Trail starts at Gabaldon Campground and follows the East Fork of the Little Colorado River; the West Baldy Trail starts at Sheep's Crossing and follows the West Fork of the Little Colorado River. The summit itself is on White Mountain Apache land and is closed to nontribal members.

Brookchar Campground

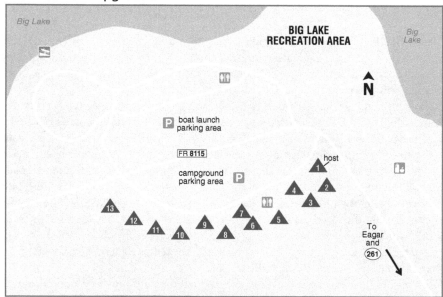

GETTING THERE

From Eagar, take AZ 260 west 3 miles to AZ 261. Turn left and drive south 18 miles to Forest Road 8115. Turn right and continue 2 miles to the campground.

GPS COORDINATES N33° 52.500' W109° 24.839'

34

East Fork Recreation Area Campgrounds

Beauty ★★★★ Privacy ★★★ Spaciousness ★★★ Quiet ★★★ Security ★★★ Cleanliness ★★★

The river runs fast and clear, racing you down the road.

Close your eyes and think of Arizona. What image comes to mind? If you imagined barren wastelands and saguaro cacti, pack your bags and call in sick, because we have something else to show you! In the heart of the White Mountains runs the Black River, a perennial tributary of the Salt River. It waters a forested Eden near Greer. You plunge into the midst of Apache-Sitgreaves National Forests, more than 2 million acres of some of the most beautiful land in the state. Once you reach the recreation area, Forest Road 276 runs with the Black River for 6 miles through a deep gorge in the pine-covered cliffs. Rock formations stained with lichen jut out between moss-draped trees, attesting to the rare abundance of moisture here. The river runs fast and clear, racing you down the road.

You can choose among six campgrounds in the East Fork Recreation Area, each within sight or sound of the river. Following a national trend to reduce campers' impact on water sources, some sites have been moved across the road, but no site in all of East Fork is more than a short walk from the stream. Former campground sites have become day-use areas where you may pull off to spend the day fishing along the banks. Trout, smallmouth bass,

The fast-flowing East Fork of the Black River

KEY INFORMATION

CONTACT: 928-339-5000, tinyurl.com/eastforkra

OPEN: May–October

SITES: 77

EACH SITE HAS: Picnic table, fire ring; some have an Adirondack shelter

ASSIGNMENT: First-come, first-served; no reservations

REGISTRATION: With camp host

AMENITIES: Vault toilets; water spigot; campground host; firewood, bearproof boxes; wheelchair-accessible sites, group sites, and day-use ramadas at Horse Springs

PARKING: At campsites

FEE: $14–$16/night, $5/additional vehicle

ELEVATION: 7,500'–7,900'

RESTRICTIONS:

PETS: On leash only

FIRES: In fire rings only

ALCOHOL: Permitted

VEHICLES: 32-foot length limit; 1 vehicle/site; ATVs prohibited in campgrounds

QUIET HOURS: 10 p.m.–6 a.m.

OTHER: 14-day stay limit; pack in/pack out; bear-country food-storage requirements; checkout 1 p.m.; discharging of firearms prohibited

and catfish all await you in the cold, rushing water. Diamond Rock, named for the distinctive rock formation just down the road, offers 12 sites in three loops. In the first loop, sites 1–6 line the river as it meanders away from the road. Dense brush guards the riverbanks here, but that won't slow a true fisherman down. Our favorite site here is number 6, at the end of the loop. Sites 7 and 8 are in the second loop, tucked back into the woods, well separated from each other. You can find a few of the Adirondack shelters originally built by the Civilian Conservation Corps in Diamond Rock: history you might use to stay dry at site 7 when the heavy monsoon rains fall in July–September.

Aspen Campground's six sites overlook a bend in the river. Sites 4–6 are the nicest here and perhaps the closest ones to the river in East Fork. Across the road at Deer Creek, check out site 5, which is very large and on its own little loop with site 6. Raccoon's 10 sites sit very close to each other and right along the road, making it the least attractive place to stay unless you're totally focused on fishing.

The largest campground of the six, Horse Springs, takes trailers up to 32 feet long. Its two loops—Polecat and Porcupine—wind through a dense pocket of ponderosa pine along a hillside below the road. The host resides at site 6 in the Porcupine loop, and sites 7 and 8 are wheelchair accessible with upright grills. Sites 10 and 12–14 sit right next to the water. In the Polecat loop, sites 18–21 back up to the river, and here 18 and 19 are the wheelchair-accessible sites. Horse Springs also offers day-use parking and a picnic area for $6, and a group-use ramada for $100 per day or $125 per night.

You've been slowly descending with the river, and soon the canyon opens into a valley. Here the road forks. If you turn left and cross the river, you arrive at the only campground on the opposite bank—Buffalo Crossing. The 16 campsites line up under the ponderosas near a green meadow filled with irises and red cinquefoils. You can hear the water cascading over small boulders, though you can't see the river through the brush. A short hike downstream takes you to an old bridge and a great view upstream and down. The best site here is 16, spacious and close to the river.

If you follow FR 25 to FR 68, you'll head up to the West Fork of the Black River. The free camping area here was closed after the Wallow Fire of 2011 due to potential hazards, but in 2017 the U.S. Forest Service (USFS) reopened a portion of the area for dispersed camping. The USFS says there are approximately 70 undefined sites here, and undefined is right! A fire ring and sometimes a picnic table are all that mark most of these sites, but you'll find a few Adirondack shelters. To get to some of the sites you need to ford the river—usually possible by passenger car—but be sure to check the water level. To get even farther away from the crowds, follow the remains of the road through the river again to get to the last and least-accessible sites

East Fork Recreation Area Campgrounds

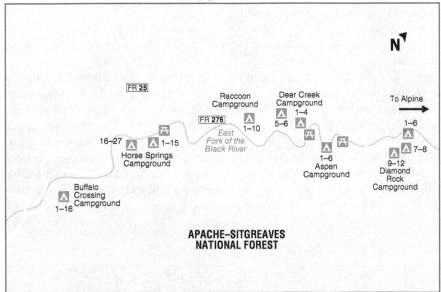

GETTING THERE

From Alpine, drive 2 miles north on US 191 to FR 249. Turn left and drive west 5 miles to FR 276. Turn left and continue south 6 miles to East Fork Recreation Area.

GPS COORDINATES N33° 49.060' W109° 18.010'

35

Honeymoon Campground

Beauty ★★★★ Privacy ★★★★★ Spaciousness ★★★★ Quiet ★★★★ Security ★★★ Cleanliness ★★★

You'll hardly see another soul while in camp.

Picture the proud groom and blushing bride (hopefully no longer in trousseau), rattling up and down precipitous mountain curves and fording cold running streams, headed for the middle of nowhere to celebrate their wedding night to the music of wind-rushed leaves and murmuring water. Apparently, that was one forest ranger's idea of the perfect honeymoon. If you agree, follow the ribbon of Upper Eagle Creek as it winds its way through the White Mountains to find this tiny gem of a campground.

From Clifton, take the Devil's Highway (the Coronado Trail) north to Forest Road 217. Don't let the thick black line on the map fool you: 25 miles per hour is as fast as you'll want to take this highway, so plan accordingly. The beauty of the Coronado Trail always makes me forget the curves, at least until I glance down and my stomach lurches into my throat. Once you turn on to Upper Eagle Creek Road, the surface turns to dirt, easily passable in a sedan as long as the roads are dry and the creek isn't running high. The 22-mile road climbs up and down through pinyon–juniper forest and into grassy plains, following sycamore-lined Eagle Creek. At least a dozen DO NOT CROSS WHEN FLOODED signs decorate the road-side, half of which are followed by the 15-foot-wide rocky stream. You pass several working ranches (and yes, that cow in front of you *does* own the road), and the Eagle School, which no longer holds classes but still serves as a community hall and polling place. As the road climbs and the valley narrows, the foliage grows more lush.

Private and pretty enough for a honeymoon

KEY INFORMATION

CONTACT: 928-687-8600, tinyurl.com
/honeymoon-camp

OPEN: Year-round when roads are open

SITES: 4

EACH SITE HAS: Picnic table, fire ring

ASSIGNMENT: First-come, first-served;
no reservations

REGISTRATION: Not required

AMENITIES: Vault toilets

PARKING: At campsites

FEE: None

ELEVATION: 5,400'

RESTRICTIONS:

PETS: On leash only

FIRES: In fire rings only

ALCOHOL: Permitted

VEHICLES: 16-foot length limit

QUIET HOURS: Not specified

OTHER: 14-day stay limit; pack in/pack out;
bear-country food-storage restrictions;
discharging of firearms prohibited; no
drinking water available

Just before the road ends at the Four Drag Ranch, the Honeymoon Campground appears on your left. The sites are right along the road, but you won't find that the traffic keeps you up at night. More likely, you'll hardly see another soul while in camp, which is part of the allure here.

The sites are not signed, but there are four picnic tables with associated fire pits that we've numbered from south to north. The first two are within sight of each other under a canopy of sycamore, cottonwood, maple, and Arizona walnut. You won't find designated pads, but plenty of flat earth will easily accommodate large tents. A set of pit toilets with a wheelchair-accessible concrete ramp separates the first two sites from the third. Site 3, a cul-de-sac with its back to a dry wash, is every bit as large and shady as the first two and affords even more privacy. All three sites are just across the road from the creek, but the bank in this area is reinforced with rough rock riprap that makes for uncertain footing. Stroll 100 yards in either direction and you can more easily reach the river's edge to try your hand at fishing.

At first glance, this appears to be the extent of the campground, but if you continue down FR 217 nearly to the ranch gate, you'll find one more campsite—this time on the creek side of the road. An immense Arizona sycamore shades the spacious site, whose only neighbors are the infrequent visitors to the nearby trailhead. As at the other sites, you have a picnic table and a metal fire ring with a flip-up grill, and it's a moderate 200-yard walk back to the toilets. This is our pick of the sites.

The campground is open year-round, but the U.S. Forest Service indicates that the best time to camp is May–September. Be prepared for afternoon rainstorms July–September and high water during the spring snowmelt. Fall is a particularly nice time to visit, when the maples and sycamores turn crimson and gold. The only time you might find a crowd here would be during hunting seasons. The forest abounds with mule deer, elk, black bears, and wild turkeys. Eagles do soar here, and Herons will fish the creek with you.

Along the same fenceline as the ranch gate you'll find the trailhead. Beyond the vehicle gate is FR 8369, an extremely primitive road that is closed from February 1 through June 30 each year. One glance at the yard-deep ruts leading into the creek convinced us we wouldn't attempt this path in anything other than a Jeep or ATV. From here you can access a network of hiking trails, including Squirrel Canyon 34, East Eagle 33, and Robinson Mesa Trail 27. Trail 33 travels a relatively flat 12.6 miles along East Eagle Creek and eventually lands you at US 191; you can use it as a connector to the Eagle National Recreation Trail, which works its way north from a point on FR 217, touches the highway near Rose Peak, and climbs north to the eastern point of the Bear Wallow Wilderness. Be sure to get information and maps from the Clifton Ranger District before heading out on any of the trails. The Eagle Creek Road runs very close to the San Carlos Apache Reservation boundary, so if you decide to strike out to the west make sure you have any permits you might need.

Honeymoon Campground

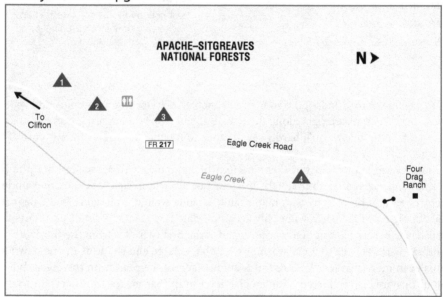

GETTING THERE

From Clifton, take US 191 north 30 miles to FR 217. Turn left and go west 22 miles to the campground.

GPS COORDINATES N33° 28.398' W109° 28.918'

36

KP Cienega Campground

Beauty ★★★★★ Privacy ★★★★ Spaciousness ★★★ Quiet ★★★★ Security ★★★ Cleanliness ★★★

The campground is set a mile back from the highway in a serene meadow.

Tiny KP Cienega is our favorite campground in one of our favorite parts of Arizona. Whether you are traveling north from the mining town of Clifton or south from Alpine, you are driving through some of the finest scenery you'll see anywhere. This route, steeped in history and superstition, has been designated the Coronado Trail Scenic Byway, and it roughly follows the northward route of Spanish explorer Francisco Vásquez de Coronado. He and his army passed this way in 1540—the first Europeans to do so—looking for the fabled Seven Cities of Cibola. Coronado never found his cities of gold, but his expedition created a legacy integral to the history of the Southwest.

Possibly the least-traveled and curviest federal highway in the nation, this road rises more than 6,000 feet in elevation over the course of 120 miles through nearly 500 switchbacks—bring your Dramamine. It was once nicknamed the Devil's Highway thanks to its original numbering: US 666. To placate fearful travelers, appease local residents, and prevent the highway signs from being stolen, the highway was officially renumbered 191 in Arizona. Don't let the superstitions scare you. Looking out at the silhouettes of the White Mountains fading into the distance, you feel more like you're headed for heaven.

Sneezeweed spreads its sunny blooms across the meadow.

KEY INFORMATION

CONTACT: 928-339-5000, tinyurl.com /kpcienega

OPEN: Full services May–September, depending on weather and road conditions

SITES: 5

EACH SITE HAS: Picnic table, fire ring

ASSIGNMENT: First-come, first-served; no reservations

REGISTRATION: Not required

AMENITIES: Vault toilets

PARKING: At campsites

FEE: None

ELEVATION: 9,000'

RESTRICTIONS:

PETS: On leash only

FIRES: In fire rings only

ALCOHOL: Permitted

VEHICLES: 16-foot length limit

QUIET HOURS: 10 p.m.–6 a.m.

OTHER: 14-day stay limit; pack in/pack out; bear-country food-storage requirements; mountain bikes prohibited in Blue Range Primitive Area; no drinking water available

The word *cienega* means "wetlands" or "marsh," and you pass a small, marshy pond as you make your way to five campsites underneath a small stand of ponderosa, spruce, and Douglas-fir. The campground is set a mile back from the highway in a serene meadow. Look for wild turkey, elk, and deer on your way in. On rare occasions, bear and even recently reintroduced Mexican gray wolves have wandered into the campground. Dainty Franciscan bluebells and wild roses line the campground road, and sneezeweed, Richardson's geraniums and towering Jacob's ladder dot the meadow. The remains of a picturesque cattle chute stands nearby, left over from the days when the area served as summer pasture for the YY Cattle Company. Look for the small plaque near the entrance to the campground honoring ranchers Toles and Lou Ella Cosper, whose relatives still meet here every June for a family reunion.

Site 1 is the first one inside the small loop, with a good view of the meadow for watching elk graze at sunset. On the outside, site 2 is compact, grassy, and open, with a pleasant view into the upper meadow. Site 3 is set back toward the trees and a little more secluded. At the back of the loop, site 4 sits up on a slight hill, also in the trees, and has a nicely shaded tent area with less of a meadow view. As you round the end of the loop, you come to the restrooms and site 5. This site inside the loop has a nice view down the length of the meadow.

All sites have picnic tables, fire rings with flip-up grills, and cut logs for sitting or setting. The campground is open year-round but may be inaccessible due to snow. This area usually gets Arizona's first and last snowfall, and temperatures can get down to the low 30s by October. At nearly 9,000 feet elevation, it is always cool in the summer. You should also be prepared for daily monsoon rains July–September.

In 2011, the Wallow Fire, the largest wildfire in Arizona's recorded history, burned through this area. The conflagration was started by a campfire left unattended; it burned for 41 days, over 538,049 acres. Dense stands of young aspens, New Mexico locust, and raspberries have sprouted under the burned spruce and firs, but there are still lots of snags (standing deadwood) and care must be taken in the burned areas. Despite the fire, you'll find spectacular hiking on the many trails that crisscross the Blue Range area of the White Mountains. The KP Cienega Trail starts at the campground and quickly descends into a canyon, crossing the KP Creek several times. A nice day hike takes you 3 miles down to the confluence where the north and south forks of KP Creek merge to form two 10-foot waterfalls. If you continue past the falls, the trail becomes significantly more difficult, but you can follow the creek on its journey to the Blue River by combining the hike with the Steeple Trail 73.

KP Cienega is normally full on weekends and often weekdays during the late spring and summer. If you can't find a spot, head just up US 191 to Hannagan Campground. Although larger and more RV friendly, it's beautifully forested and well maintained. Nearby Hannagan Meadow Lodge offers room and cabin rentals and runs a general store with gas, simple groceries, and souvenirs. The small restaurant primarily serves lodge guests, but if you'd like a pleasant home-cooked meal, call or stop in and make a reservation ahead of time so they'll know how much food to prepare. For a truly southwestern experience, saddle up at Chuck's Trail Riding Adventures for a guided horseback-riding tour. The lodge porch is a great place to watch the hummingbirds and spy on elk grazing serenely at sunrise or sunset in Hannagan Meadow.

KP Cienega Campground

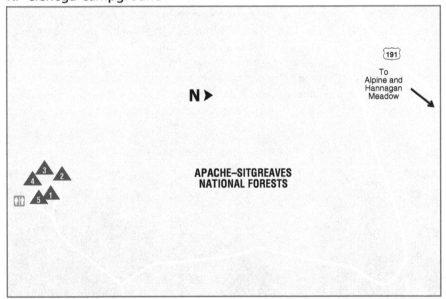

GETTING THERE

From Alpine, take US 191 south 27 miles. Turn left at the KP CIENEGA sign and head east 1.3 miles to the campground.

GPS COORDINATES N33° 35.063' W109° 21.602'

37

⛺ Los Burros Campground

Beauty ★★★★ Privacy ★★★ Spaciousness ★★★★ Quiet ★★★ Security ★★★ Cleanliness ★★★★

In a land of lakes and streams, a campground away from the water can be a quiet oasis.

Los Burros is just a few miles north of the bustling lakes of the White Mountain Apache Reservation, but your fishing tackle can stay packed here. Instead, the campground looks out of the tall pines on a lovely grassy meadow. In 1909, the U.S. Forest Service (USFS) set aside 240 acres here for a fire guard, and Los Burros was home to the ranger who rode out daily to man Lake Mountain Lookout, watching for the telltale thread of smoke that would call out brave men to fight forest fires with hand axes and shovels. Later the timber sales agent for the area shared the ranger's quarters, and the meadow and spring served as a camp for lumbermen feeding the mill at McNary, as well as for cowboys and sheepherders moving their stock through the area. Don Hansen, who farmed nearby Reservation Flat in the 1920s and 1930s, remembered one USFS employee by the name of Rogers, whose lovely and musical daughters brought an added attraction to the meadow. Les Joslin quotes him in *Uncle Sam's Cabins:* "All the boys in the country knew where Los Burros was."

The historic Ranger Station still stands, awaiting restoration, along with a barn and corral, and has been added to the National Register of Historic Places. This site was chosen for a station in part due to the nearby perennial spring, now capped. The meadow, which served as a pasture for the rangers' horses, now attracts an abundance of wildlife, including black bear, mule deer, pronghorn antelope, and Merriam's turkey. Elk frequently visit here, especially during the fall rut, so listen for the males' bugle call. This is a popular spot for

Rangers stabled their sturdy mounts in the barn at Los Burros starting in 1909.

KEY INFORMATION

CONTACT: 928-368-2100, tinyurl.com
/losburros

OPEN: Full services May–October, depending
on weather and road conditions

SITES: 12

EACH SITE HAS: Picnic table, fire ring

ASSIGNMENT: First-come, first-served;
no reservations

REGISTRATION: Not required

AMENITIES: Vault toilet, corrals,
campground host

PARKING: At campsites

FEE: None

ELEVATION: 7,900'

RESTRICTIONS:

PETS: On leash only

FIRES: In fire rings only

ALCOHOL: Permitted

VEHICLES: 22-foot length limit

QUIET HOURS: 10 p.m.–6 a.m.

OTHER: 14-day stay limit; pack in/pack out;
no water

other large mammals as well: horseback riders, mountain bikers, and hikers come to the Los Burros Trail, a 13-mile loop through mixed ponderosa and aspen forest with a moderate elevation change of 500 feet. The trail is part of the White Mountains Trail System, a series of 11 interconnected loop trails in the Lakeside Ranger District built and maintained by volunteers from the community. A short side trip takes you to the top of Lake Mountain and the fire tower, where you can see all the way to the San Francisco Peaks.

Forest Road 224 is graded gravel, but at the turn into Los Burros the gravel gives way to rutted dirt that turns muddy in the late summer rains and spring snowmelt. The managed season is May–October and the road is not maintained for winter travel, although the campground is open year-round for the intrepid and well prepared.

The meadow is on your right as you enter the campground. The three large, open sites closest to the meadow best accommodate campers with horses, and two small corrals stand between sites 11 and 12. These sites have great views, if little shade. Spacious site 10 is reserved for the campground host. The road forms a rough loop, with sites 8 and 9 and the trailhead at the end. Inside the loop, sites 4 and 7 also have a view, and a nice oak partially shades site 4. The rest of the sites lie inside the tree line and are well shaded. Sites 5 and 6 have sizable tent areas, and site 2 is set back from the rest with some undergrowth for privacy. All have steel fire rings with flip-up grills and metal picnic tables, and there's a vault toilet between site 6 and the trailhead. Parking is at the sites, but trailhead parking on a busy day might encroach on site 8.

The campground is rarely full and mostly used by folks enjoying the cool temperatures or accessing the trail system. When we visited we met a gentleman who spends most of his summer camping throughout the White Mountains with his dogs to get away from the summer heat; a family on horseback with two small children who could have been born in the saddle; and three women who had trailered their mounts all the way from Tucson just to ride the Los Burros Trail.

Los Burros makes a good base camp for exploring the White Mountains and Apache-Sitgreaves National Forests. Unpack your tackle and head south to fish for the native Apache trout, found only in Arizona. Thanks to the conservation policies of the White Mountain tribe, sportsmen can once again angle for this endangered fish. Stop at the Hon-Dah Resort and Casino for more information about recreational regulations in the Fort Apache Indian Reservation and to purchase permits (for details see profile 40, Pacheta Lake Campground, page 145).

Full amenities can be found just to the west in the picturesque towns of Lakeside and Pinetop. The two towns have grown together and have groceries, gas, gifts, restaurants, and rental cabins. If Los Burros has left you with the urge to cowboy a bit, you'll find several riding stables in the area.

Los Burros Campground

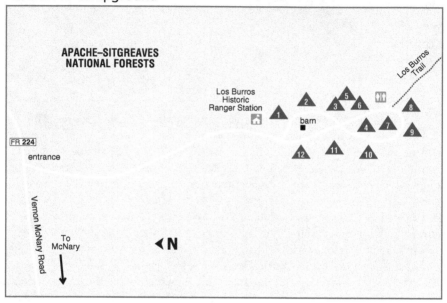

GETTING THERE

From McNary, take FR 224 north 7 miles to the campground sign. Turn right and drive 0.25 mile to the campground.

GPS COORDINATES N34° 08.738' W109° 46.658'

38

Lower Juan Miller Campground

Beauty ★★★★ Privacy ★★★★ Spaciousness ★★★ Quiet ★★★★ Security ★★ Cleanliness ★★

This verdant Eden is one of the quietest spots in Arizona.

Drive US 191 north through the eastern part of the state and you're exposed to a slice of the vast diversity that makes up the state of Arizona. The road rises from the scrubby floor of the San Simon Valley into the heart of Arizona's copper country. As you climb, you pass through the vast, open-pit copper mines of Morenci and Clifton. The mountains have been transformed into inverted pyramids of marbled horizontal shelves. It's hard not to stare in both horror and awe at the raw kaleidoscope of peach, rust, sage, and slate gray. Beyond the mines, you see the mountains as they looked before their minerals were dug out—rugged, rocky hills dotted green with juniper and pinyon pine. The higher the elevation, the lower the air temperature becomes. Soon you can turn off the air-conditioning and roll down the windows; perhaps the fresh air will help the impending motion sickness as you take another sharp turn around the next switchback.

After 27 miles of breathtaking views and heart-stopping drops, which have probably taken more than an hour to navigate, you reach the turn for Juan Miller Road. Two tiny campgrounds patiently wait for anyone willing to come this far to visit. Upper Juan Miller comes first, and the tight stream crossing easily weeds out the unadventurous and the ponderous. Arizona has so many lovely campgrounds dating from the Civilian Conservation

The perfect place to begin a long day exploring the Blue River

KEY INFORMATION

CONTACT: 928-687-8600, tinyurl.com /lowerjuanmiller

OPEN: Year-round, weather permitting

SITES: 4

EACH SITE HAS: Picnic table, fire ring

ASSIGNMENT: First-come, first-served; no reservations

REGISTRATION: Not required

AMENITIES: Vault toilets

PARKING: At campsites

FEE: None

ELEVATION: 5,700'

RESTRICTIONS:

PETS: Permitted

FIRES: In fire ring only

ALCOHOL: Permitted

VEHICLES: 16-foot length limit; RVs not recommended

QUIET HOURS: Not specified

OTHER: 14-day stay limit; no drinking water available

Corps era that it comes as no surprise to find their mark in this verdant Eden as well; four sites in a tight loop graced by charming stonework blend into the hilly, uneven ground. The dense undergrowth and lack of good tent spots make this green gem far more suitable for picnics than camping.

Continue the short distance to Lower Juan Miller, which has more room to spread out. The campground consists of only four designated sites, but there are also some suitable dispersed areas; it's unlikely you will ever find this rarely used campground full. Mature Gambel oak, ponderosa pine, and alligator juniper provide an emerald canopy over the entire scene, and the bed of Juan Miller Creek boasts giant-leaved sycamores. The creek was dry when we visited, but the greenery attests to the abundant moisture available here. In the fall, the leaves create a panorama of gold and russet. Traffic patterns within the campground are hard to discern, but you'll find plenty of space to park. Site 1 has small tent areas close to the picnic table and larger options a few steps away. Site 2 is roomy, but sits right in the middle of the camp area. We prefer site 3, set apart from the others at the end of the line with shrub live oak and velvet ash providing some screening. Shady site 4 backs up to the creekbed and would be very pleasant when the creek is flowing. Be prepared for afternoon thunderstorms during the monsoon months of July–September and for chilly evenings even during the middle of summer.

Stonework picnic tables grace each site, along with metal or stone fire rings. The campground feels a bit neglected, with elderly vault toilets and obviously ineffectual cattle fencing (watch your step), but the 16-foot length limit and twisty mountain roads discourage RV traffic. You may find more neighbors here in hunting season than at any other time, since the White Mountains abound with game, including deer, elk, and the occasional black bear or mountain lion. Juan Miller is a quiet place. Catch it without other occupants and you may find it one of the quietest spots in Arizona.

The Juan Miller Road, campgrounds, and creek are named for an early settler who emigrated from Germany and homesteaded in the Blue River area. According to records his name was von Müellar, but locals accustomed to Spanish and English names presumably rechristened him. The road continues 12 miles past the campground, descending to meet the Blue River near the historic XXX Ranch (not what it sounds like to modern ears—that was rancher Fred Fritz's cattle brand). A cold, tumbling trout stream, the perennial Blue is one of Arizona's most beautiful rivers. The isolation of this rare river access makes it a wonderful fishing spot. The Blue is not a runnable river most of the year, but lucky kayakers with good timing might catch the spring snowmelt. In warmer weather when the water is lower, you can hike upstream toward the Blue Range Primitive Area, 173,762 acres of unmarred wilderness with miles of hiking and horseback-riding trails. Hiking this mountainous terrain is strenuous, since you're either going up or down with every step, but it's incredibly rewarding. This valley has a long history, and with a little exploration you may find evidence of occupation from the heyday of cattle ranching all the way back to Puebloan times.

The Juan Millers also make a good stop before exploring farther up the Coronado Highway. For more information about the area, see profile 36, KP Cienega Campground (page 123), and contact Apache-Sitgreaves National Forests.

Lower Juan Miller Campground

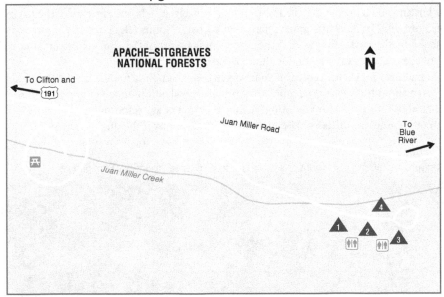

GETTING THERE

From Clifton, take US 191 north 27 miles to FR 475/Juan Miller Road. Turn right and drive east 2 miles to the campground.

GPS COORDINATES N33° 16.157' W109° 20.662'

39

Lyman Lake State Park Campground

Beauty ★★★ Privacy ★★★ Spaciousness ★★★★ Quiet ★★★ Security ★★★★ Cleanliness ★★★★

The whole area has a wide-open high desert feel, with few trees and a big, big sky.

North of the White Mountains, the land turns to high desert plains: rolling, grassy hills and nothing for miles but dotted dark shapes resolving into junipers or cows as you approach. A rise or dip in the road may suddenly reveal a rugged wash or outcrop flashing past, then just waving grass, stubby pinyons, and sky again. Hidden back in a rocky bowl in those rolling hills is 1,500-acre Lyman Lake, centerpiece of the oldest recreational state park in Arizona.

As you drive into the park, you pass the dam that creates this reservoir on the Little Colorado River, whose watershed drains the highest northern slopes of the White Mountains, including Escudilla Mountain and Mount Baldy. Look down into the muddy pond to your left and you'll usually see turtles sunning themselves. A former feature of the park was a herd of "wild" buffalo that grazed here, owned by St. Johns Chamber of Commerce and managed by the park. They're sadly gone now, but traces of their presence remain on the logo of the general store and on the Buffalo Trail.

Stop at the tiny visitor center on your way in to pick up information on boating and hiking, learn about the park's flora and fauna, browse a collection of books to read and return, or chat about how the fish are biting. Although rangers are often out and about on duty, summer volunteers will assist. Use the self-registration box if the office is closed.

Petroglyphs and pueblo ruins: signs of ancient lives that still speak to today's Hopi people

KEY INFORMATION

CONTACT: 928-337-4441, azstateparks.com/lyman-lake

OPEN: Year-round

SITES: 56

EACH SITE HAS: Picnic table, fire ring, some have an upright grill, some have a shelter, some have electrical hookups

ASSIGNMENT: First-come, first-served; reservations accepted for group sites and cabins

REGISTRATION: Purchase daily and annual passes at the park office; on-site self-registration when office is closed

AMENITIES: Flush toilets, hot showers, water spigots, boat ramp, beach, day-use area, nature trails, cabins, dump station, group sites, resident park manager, firewood, wheelchair-accessible sites, fish-cleaning stations, fishing docks, ice, general store, paddle boat rentals

PARKING: At campsites

FEE: $20/night no hookups, $28/night water/electric, $33/night water/electric/sewer, $15/additional vehicle; $5 online-reservation fee

ELEVATION: 6,000'

RESTRICTIONS:

PETS: On leash only

FIRES: In fire rings only

ALCOHOL: Permitted

VEHICLES: No length limit; ATVs prohibited; 2 vehicles/site

QUIET HOURS: 10 p.m.–7 a.m.

OTHER: Discharging of firearms prohibited; firewood gathering prohibited; checkout time for camping 12 p.m.; checkout time for cabins 10 a.m.; removing plants, animals, or archaeological, geological, or historical objects prohibited

If you don't feel like roughing it, you can rent eight cabins that sport porches with lake views and come complete with electricity and climate control. If you're just fine with your own tent, you'll find plenty of good spots. The B loop has no hookups and consists of five sites among scattered junipers up on the hillside. You can see the lake from here, over the RV sites. If this suits you, go for 26B, a private corner site with a 180° lake view. Each B site comes with a small steel ramada shading the picnic table, an upright grill, and fire pit. Tent spots throughout the campground tend to be rocky, but level. The whole area has a wide-open high desert feel, with few trees and a big, big sky.

You can skip sites 18–25, where the RVs line up like giant piglets, and head down toward sites 17–15. These three sites rank among our favorites, set apart from the rest of the loop with mostly unobstructed views of the lake. You'll discover several more fine sites along the loop nearest to the lake, as long as you don't mind being part of your neighbors' lake view. For more privacy, head to the other side of the campground. You're farther from the lake here, especially back at sites 34, 36, and 38, but you may find it more peaceful. Many of the sites have solidly built brick ramadas for relief from the glaring summer sun or pounding monsoon rains. They also have hookups, but the park rangers will usually allow tenters to camp at the lower price.

One of the nicest things about this park is that you're allowed to pitch your tent right on the beach below the cabins. Camping used to be available farther along the shoreline, but due to tree damage and waste problems, those areas are now day use only. The main beach area is convenient to the restrooms, and a ramada and a couple of picnic tables are available for early birds. If you really don't feel like roughing it, there are eight rental cabins that sport porches with lake views and come complete with electricity and climate control.

Prime time for water sports occurs between Memorial Day and Labor Day. Lyman Lake touts itself as one of the smoothest waterskiing lakes in Arizona and one of the few lakes in the area to have no boat-size restrictions; it even comes complete with its own slalom course. Other parts have been designated as no-wake zones for anglers trying to lure channel catfish and largemouth bass from the depths below.

The park is open every day of the year, and the off-season can be a good time to catch some peace and quiet on the lake. Even if it's too cold to swim, there are plenty of things to do during the cooler months, when the fishing and the hiking may be at their best. Trails include the Peninsula Petroglyph Trail, a 0.25-mile hike up a rocky hill where passing ancients etched numerous signs and symbols into the rock. In season, don't miss the ranger-guided boat tour to an even more spectacular site across the lake at the Ultimate Petroglyph Trail. Guided tours are also available of Rattlesnake Pointe Pueblo, a partially excavated 80- to 90-room village dating from the 1300s.

Lyman Lake State Park Campground

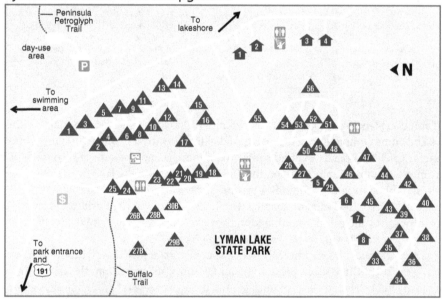

GETTING THERE

From Springerville, take US 191 north 18 miles to the park entrance. Turn right into park.

GPS COORDINATES N34° 21.783' W109° 23.173'

40

Pacheta Lake Campground

Beauty ★★★★ Privacy ★★★★★ Spaciousness ★★★ Quiet ★★★★ Security ★★ Cleanliness ★★

Early in the morning, the trees are reflected in a perfect mirror of water, with the silence broken only by birdsong and perhaps the swish of a fly rod.

The Apache term *Hon-Dah* is often translated as "be my guest," and it's an apt name for the small resort town at the crossroads of the Fort Apache reservation. The ancestral land of the White Mountain Apache, the reservation ranges from the stark beauty of the Salt River Canyon to the majestic cloud-swathed peak of Mount Baldy. The tribe welcomes visitors to Arizona's greenest, most hospitable region, a patchwork of forested mountains and blue lakes crisscrossed with perennial streams.

Fishing is one of the region's main attractions, and the campgrounds on the reservation are all associated with one of the many lakes and streams. These areas see considerable use by both visitors and tribal members, but a few more primitive, harder to reach areas are seldom busy; one of these is Pacheta Lake.

You'll find Pacheta on the eastern side of the reservation, past popular 280-acre Reservation Lake and much smaller Drift Fence Lake. The road on to Pacheta begins as a good dirt road that gets considerably worse—four-wheel drive isn't necessary, but a high-clearance vehicle is recommended. Keep your eyes open for loose cattle everywhere on the reservation, even in the campgrounds.

The lushness of the White Mountains surrounds you at Pacheta.

KEY INFORMATION

CONTACT: 928-338-4346,
wmatoutdoors.org

OPEN: Year-round; full services
mid-May–Labor Day

SITES: 7

EACH SITE HAS: Picnic table, fire ring

ASSIGNMENT: First-come, first-served;
no reservations

REGISTRATION: Camping permit required;
purchase through the White Mountain
Apache Tribe at the website above

AMENITIES: Vault toilets

PARKING: At campsites

FEE: $9/day/vehicle for camping, $9/person/
day for fishing, $9/day/vehicle for outdoor
recreation permit

ELEVATION: 8,500'

RESTRICTIONS:

PETS: On leash only

FIRES: In fire rings only

ALCOHOL: Permitted

VEHICLES: ATVs prohibited; RVs
not recommended

QUIET HOURS: Not specified

OTHER: No firearms; swimming prohibited;
no drinking water available; bear-country
food-storage requirements

Ponderosa, Douglas-fir, blue spruce, and a few aspens surround the small, 68-acre lake. Large boulders covered in lichen scatter the rocky shoreline, reminding us of northern Minnesota. Camping is restricted to designated areas, but the campsites themselves are not so clearly distinguished. In other, busier reservation campgrounds, tents and small RVs populate any spot that can accommodate them. At Pacheta Lake, the official number of campsites is 15, but we mapped seven clearly defined sites. Each site has a picnic table and a stone fire ring. Signs forbid moving the tables, but you will find that some have wandered away to other sites. The latrines are antique and of questionable construction, but are thoughtfully placed with entrances facing the woods, providing great views if the door is no longer attached. Gaps between the wooden planks provide good ventilation. Be prepared to BYOTP.

There's an informality to the Pacheta Lake arrangements, but you're well compensated for any inconveniences. Some of the sites are along the shoreline, allowing you to park your canoe or kickboat practically in your camp. Early in the morning, the trees are reflected in a perfect mirror of water, with the silence broken only by birdsong and perhaps the swish of a fly rod. Site 1 is generously sized and right on the water. Next around the loop, site 2 sits on the bank above the trickling stream that feeds the lake and is an excellent site for birdwatching. Up a slope from the lake, site 3 offers a bit more shade and privacy. Site 6 is small but has a lovely view. Also on the water, site 7 is the most private of all. This area is abundant in wildlife, so practice campsite food safety and be aware that Mexican gray wolves have been introduced in nearby areas of the Apache-Sitgreaves National Forests and are present on the reservation.

Pacheta Lake is stocked with brown and rainbow trout, for catch and release only. You do not need an Arizona fishing license here, but if you don't belong to the White Mountain Apache Tribe, you will need a tribal permit for *any* recreational activity, including picnicking and driving anywhere off the main paved roads. The Apache take the use and preservation of their land seriously—be sure to get the necessary permits and follow the rules. Regulations and permits are available at Hon-Dah Ski and Outdoor Sport, at the tribal office in Whiteriver, at a few stores in neighboring towns, and from Sportsman's Warehouse in

Phoenix and Tucson. During the summer, you can also buy permits at Sunrise Lake Marina. Pacheta Lake is serviced from mid-May through Labor Day. You may camp at Pacheta outside of the season, but you will have to pack out your trash.

For a lovely drive through canyon views and forested mountains, take uncrowded Y55 from Pacheta Lake to Whiteriver, but beware of logging trucks during the workweek. Make a stop at the White Mountain Apache Cultural Center and Museum at Fort Apache Historic Park. The White Mountain Apache provided many of the scouts who assisted the US Cavalry during the Apache Wars, and here you can learn more about the tribe's unique culture and history.

If you visit the White Mountains during the summer, you may want to catch a local rodeo. Like many of the Southwest's Native Americans, the Apache are skillful and enthusiastic cowboys. The major event of the year, the Tribal Fair and Rodeo, occurs Labor Day weekend. Summer also offers scenic lift rides at Sunrise Ski Resort, but this playground really comes alive in winter.

Pacheta Lake Campground

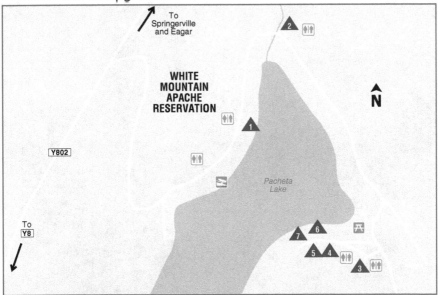

GETTING THERE

From Whiteriver, take Y55 east 40 miles to Y802. Turn left and follow the signs 1.8 miles to the campground.

Alternate route: From Springerville/Eagar, take US 260 west 3 miles to US 261. Turn left and drive south past Big Lake to Forest Road 249E. Turn right and continue west 5.5 miles to FR 116. Head south 7 miles to the reservation border to Y8. Drive 7 miles southwest past Reservation Lake and Drift Fence Lake to Y802. Turn left and follow the signs 1.8 miles to the campground.

GPS COORDINATES N33° 46.742' W109° 32.590'

SOUTHERN ARIZONA

An army of saguaros marches through Alamo Canyon (see next page).

41

Alamo Canyon Primitive Campground

Beauty ★★★★ Privacy ★★★★ Spaciousness ★★★★ Quiet ★★★★★ Security ★★★ Cleanliness ★★★★

At night an astonishing blanket of stars unrolls above you.

One image, one distinctive silhouette, embodies the desert Southwest for people across the globe. From cheesy tourist tchotchkes to the Arizona state quarter, the mighty saguaro cactus raises its arms on high. Arizona has more than one spectacular giant, however, and the extreme southern edge of the state is the one place in the United States where you can admire the massive organ pipe cactus.

Organ Pipe Cactus National Monument preserves and celebrates more than just these prickly behemoths. Plants from four distinctive vegetation zones comingle within the park, with upland and lowland species meeting wanderers from the Gulf Coast normally exclusive to Mexico. Many animals have also adapted to this sere and severe environment, including desert bighorn sheep and critically endangered Sonoran pronghorn antelope.

Unfortunately, one of the first questions we hear when Organ Pipe is mentioned is "Is it safe?" The park shares its southern border with Mexico, and El Camino del Diablo, or the Devil's Highway, has been part of an east–west route across this almost waterless land since human beings first set foot here. Given its ominous name by Spanish explorers, marked

An organ pipe cactus reaches for a crag of the Ajo Mountains.

KEY INFORMATION

CONTACT: 520-387-6849, nps.gov/orpi

OPEN: Year-round

SITES: 4

EACH SITE HAS: Picnic table, upright grill

ASSIGNMENT: First-come, first-served; no reservations

REGISTRATION: Self-register on-site; credit cards accepted

AMENITIES: Vault toilets, nature trails, safety call button

PARKING: At campsites

FEE: $12/night plus $25/week park-entrance fee

ELEVATION: 2,300'

RESTRICTIONS:

PETS: On leash only, prohibited on some trails; permitted only on Alamo Canyon, Visitor Center Nature Trail, Palo Verde and Twin Peaks Campground perimeter trail; prohibited in backcountry

FIRES: Ground fires and wood fires prohibited

ALCOHOL: Permitted

VEHICLES: 25-foot length limit; motor homes and trailers prohibited; tent, pickup camper, and vans only; generator use is prohibited

QUIET HOURS: 10 p.m.–6 a.m.

OTHER: 7-day stay limit; discharging of firearms prohibited; firewood gathering prohibited; 5-person limit/site; checkout time is 11 a.m.; bicycles prohibited on foot trails and in backcountry; no drinking water available at the campground

and unmarked graves of travelers from every era dot the trail. Desperados and the simply desperate still travel this road, and increased enforcement in developed areas has pushed more and more traffic in drugs and human labor into remote regions, further imperiling the delicate wilderness the park was established to protect. The park's visitor center is named for Kris Eggle, a ranger who lost his life confronting drug runners; stop and read his story on the memorial sign near the entrance.

After the National Park Service constructed a heavy-duty vehicle barrier along 23 miles of the park border, illicit vehicle traffic through the backcountry has almost stopped, and the long, slow process of recovery has begun for some of the seriously impacted wilderness. With a modicum of awareness and good sense you'll have a safe and enjoyable visit.

As you are pulling into the park on AZ 85, look for the turn for Alamo Canyon Road on the east side of the highway at milepost 65.5. The turn is not signed, so go slowly and keep your eyes peeled. Drive 3 miles down a good dirt road to four campsites at the foot of the Ajo Range, whose rugged face glows crimson at sunset due to the rhyolite in the hills. All sites have a picnic table and upright grill, and saguaros and organ pipe cacti tower around you. The pick is spacious site 4, with a great view into Alamo Canyon. At night, an astonishing blanket of stars unrolls above you. From this campground you can explore the 1-mile Alamo Canyon Trail. An old ranch house, corrals, and ancient metates testify to centuries of history in the quiet and relatively verdant canyon.

If the campground is full, don't fret—there's still an opportunity to tent camp in peace. The 208-site Twin Peaks Campground near the visitor center offers water, flush toilets, solar showers, and is hosted in the winter. At the far end, the outermost two rows are designated exclusively for tent campers, with the desert as their backyard, and two more generator-free rows separate the larger RVs from the tents. Ocotillo, cholla, and brittlebush abound between sites and stately saguaros and organ pipe cacti stand here and there like sentinels; you'll find several nice spots despite the tightly packed arrangement.

When you first arrive, check in at the visitor center. Your entrance permit is valid for seven consecutive days, and if you have an interagency pass, the fee is waived. Chat with the rangers, pick up information about park activities, browse the books in the gift shop, and check the calendar of ranger patio talks, guided hikes, and van tours.

One of the best ways to explore the park is via Ajo Mountain Drive. The 21-mile self-guided loop tour highlights plants indigenous to this area and clues you in to the origins of geologic and geographic features. If you have a high-clearance vehicle, you can drive the Puerto Blanco Loop. There are few amenities; however, you can access several hiking trails and learn about historic sites, including the spring at Quitobaquito, which is home to the endangered pupfish and Sonoyta mud turtle. It is recommended that you budget 4 hours for this 37-mile dirt road loop. Among the several hikes in the park, you can also hike the 3.1-mile round-trip Estes Canyon–Bull Pasture Trails for panoramic views and possibly a sighting of bighorn sheep or javelina. Backcountry camping permits are available at the visitor center for $5.

From May to September, daytime temperatures often reach into triple digits, so most visitors come from October through April. Expect Alamo Canyon sites to fill up early in winter months.

Alamo Canyon Primitive Campground

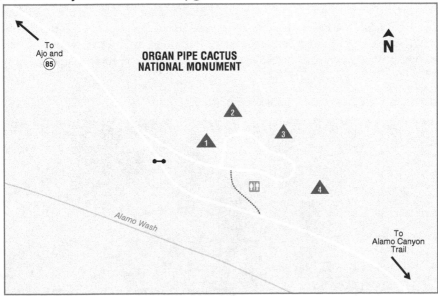

GETTING THERE

From Ajo, take AZ 85 south 23 miles; then turn left and drive 3 more miles to reach the campground at the end of the road.

GPS COORDINATES N32° 05.473' W112° 46.490'

42

Bog Springs Campground

Beauty ★★★★ Privacy ★★★ Spaciousness ★★★ Quiet ★★★★ Security ★★★★ Cleanliness ★★★★

Rare birds can be seen in this riparian oasis.

Bring your binoculars and field guide, because this is the place to go for world-famous bird-watching. At the base of the Santa Rita Mountains, with Mount Wrightson towering 9,453 feet above, Bog Springs Campground is a bird-watcher's haven set among yucca, oak, and alligator juniper. Riparian Madera Canyon is close enough to Mexico that birds rarely seen north of the border, such as the elegant trogon, visit here during the breeding season. Once heavily logged—*madera* is Spanish for "timber"—the forest now hosts more than 240 species, including the magnificent hummingbird, the Montezuma quail, and even the rare eared quetzal.

Bog Springs Campground is open year-round but hosted only during winter months. Come early in the day in April and May, since the campground routinely fills up when migrating birds are in breeding plumage. The 13 sites are arranged in a one-way loop on a hillside, with the first site you come to, site 11, being the flattest and most accessible site. Site 12, set well below the road in the oaks, provides three good tenting possibilities, while site 13, near the Bog and Kent Springs Trailhead, sits on a pair of leveled pads on a steeper slope. Inside of the loop, site 8 has a bit of a view of Green Valley below, but the tent area at site 9 seems to be on the trail to the restrooms. Site 7, at the end of the loop, can accommodate a large RV, but also offers a good tent spot next to the picnic table. Near the restrooms and trailhead parking area, a short flight of steps leads down to three shady sites. Site 6 has a well-built tent pad, and sites 4 and 5 are close enough together to accommodate a larger

Don't leave your tent without binoculars and a birding guide!

KEY INFORMATION

CONTACT: 520-281-2296, tinyurl.com /bogspringscampground

OPEN: Year-round

SITES: 13

EACH SITE HAS: Picnic table, fire ring, bearproof box, some have water spigots, some have bearproof trash containers

ASSIGNMENT: First-come, first-served; no reservations

REGISTRATION: Self-register on-site

AMENITIES: Vault toilets, water spigots, campground host

PARKING: At campsites

FEE: $10/night; $10 day use

ELEVATION: 5,200'

RESTRICTIONS:

PETS: On leash only

FIRES: In fire rings only

ALCOHOL: Permitted

VEHICLES: 22-foot length limit; 2 vehicles/site

QUIET HOURS: Not specified

OTHER: 14-day stay limit; bear-country food-storage restrictions; firearms prohibited; 10-person limit/site; horses prohibited

group, but not too close for single families. Across the road, sites 2 and 3 combine to make a proper double, with two picnic tables, two fire pits, and a shared bearproof box—good for groups or two families camping together. Site 1, compact and rocky, is just across the Dutch John Spring Trail. The host's trailer is in a separate area, across the camp road from site 4.

Even if bird-watching isn't your thing, the area is rich with other opportunities. Stop at the gatehouse on your way to the campground and pick up a brochure describing local hikes. It's published by the Friends of Madera Canyon, a nonprofit organization that helps the U.S. Forest Service maintain the local trails and preserve the canyon. The group has also provided great display maps at the two trailheads in the campground. The Dutch John Spring Trail climbs 1,200 feet in a little less than 2 miles through sycamores and unusually large oaks to two springs. The Bog Springs and Kent Spring Trails begin together near site 13 and can be combined to make a nice 4.5-mile loop along a creek. Drive up to the Mount Wrightson Picnic Area for the difficult 10.8-mile Old Baldy Trail all the way to the peak of Mount Wrightson; 32 switchbacks on the last stretch will make you work for the 360° view. If you don't have an interagency pass, there's a $10 day-use fee per vehicle.

If you want to treat yourself to a night under a roof, the Santa Rita Lodge offers rental cabins, as well as guided bird tours and benches to watch our feathered friends at the bird feeders. Head a little farther south on I-19 to reach the Whipple Observatory via the Mount Hopkins scenic drive. This partnership between the Smithsonian Institution and University of Arizona offers day-long tours of one of the world's largest optical telescopes. Reservations are required for tours, but you can stop at the visitor center any weekday. If you plan your trip well, you can catch one of their star parties, when amateur astronomers set up dozens of telescopes, some homemade, to share the moon, planets, and other galaxies with you.

Box Canyon Road scenic drive will take you across the mountains to AZ 83. From here, you can reach the 14.3-mile Santa Rita section of the Arizona Trail, a network of trails beginning at the Mexican border and traversing Arizona lengthwise. The mountains also offer spelunking opportunities in Onyx Cave and the Cave of the Bells. Both caves require permits and advance reservations to enter and are not for beginning cavers.

Down AZ 83 lies Sonoita. This tiny town, which is not much more than you can see from the four-way stop, is known for its wine. You may be surprised to learn that the soil in this part of Arizona is remarkably similar to the Burgundy region of France, and several successful wineries (which all host tours and tastings) have sprouted up here. This is yet another unique landscape in Arizona; a Hollywood producer thought these rolling, grassy hills looked more like the Midwest than the Midwest itself, and the movie *Oklahoma!* was filmed here. Complete your southern Arizona tour with a stop in Patagonia to cruise the art galleries, stroll through the oldest cottonwoods in the state at Patagonia–Sonoita Creek Preserve, have a slice of pizza at the Velvet Elvis Pizza Company, and take a guided bird-watching boat tour at Patagonia Lake State Park.

Bog Springs Campground

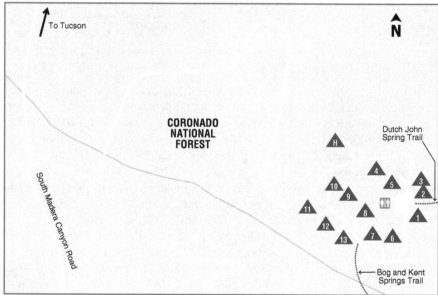

GETTING THERE

From Tucson, take I-19 south 24 miles to Continental Road/Madera Canyon exit (Exit 63). Turn left and drive 1 mile to South White House Canyon Road/South Madera Canyon Road. Turn right and continue southeast 11 miles to the campground entrance. Turn left and drive 0.5 mile to the campground.

GPS COORDINATES N31° 43.652' W110° 52.842'

43

Fourmile Canyon Campground

Beauty ★★★ Privacy ★★★★ Spaciousness ★★★★ Quiet ★★★★ Security ★★★ Cleanliness ★★★★

The best waterside hike in Arizona lies nearby.

Boxed by mountains and surrounded by wilderness, Fourmile Canyon Campground serves as a terrific base to explore some of Arizona's lesser-known natural treasures. Turn off Pinal Highway (US 70) and onto Klondyke Road. Gravel crunches under your tires as you cross ridged and crumpled badlands between the Pinaleños and Santa Theresa Mountains, then descend to the grassy floor of lower Aravaipa Canyon to meet Bonita–Klondyke Road.

Two hopeful prospectors just back from the Yukon gold rush named the town of Klondyke. Although it never yielded the riches of its Canadian namesake, nearby mines produced enough copper, silver, and lead to support more than 500 people. As the mines closed in the 1950s and ranching became less and less profitable, Klondyke's population declined. The sign at the outskirts of town now reads POP. 5. Today the town's main attraction is the Klondyke Horsehead Lodge, a popular rest stop for hikers.

At the Klondyke Bureau of Land Management (BLM) Ranger Station, turn left and drive 0.5 mile to the campground. Ten sites are arranged in a valley in the foothills of the Galiuro Mountains. Mesquites 15–20 feet tall surround you, providing some shade during hot summer mornings and afternoons. Lighted flush toilets and running water conveniently situated in the middle of the ring of sites add an extra touch of comfort. Undergrowth is

Aravaipa Canyon is one of Arizona's rarest gems—a pristine riparian hike.

KEY INFORMATION

CONTACT: 928-348-4400, blm.gov/visit
/fourmile-canyon-campground

OPEN: Year-round

SITES: 10 plus overflow

EACH SITE HAS: Picnic table, fire ring

ASSIGNMENT: First-come, first-served;
no reservations

REGISTRATION: Self-register on-site

AMENITIES: Flush toilets, water spigots,
drinking fountains

PARKING: At campsites

FEE: $5/night; $5 day use

ELEVATION: 3,500'

RESTRICTIONS:

PETS: On leash only; pets prohibited in
the wilderness

FIRES: In fire rings only; cutting firewood
from standing live or dead vegetation
prohibited

ALCOHOL: Permitted

VEHICLES: 30-foot length limit;
2 vehicles/site

QUIET HOURS: 10 p.m.–6 a.m.

OTHER: 14-day stay limit; discharging of
firearms prohibited; cleaning game in
campground prohibited; checkout 2 p.m.

---

sparse, but a bit thicker on the east side in sites 6–10. The ground at most sites is sandy and soft, but watch for rocky patches. Each site has a sturdy concrete picnic table, a hearth with a grill, and at least a couple of tent spots. The only exception is site 10, which is better suited for campers who sleep in their vehicle.

For shade and good screening, check out sites 5, 8, and 9, but be aware that if the campground is full, you may get some restroom traffic nearby. If you're with a larger party, sites 1 and 3 combine nicely, and site 7 provides several tent possibilities. Site 6 is nice for dry weather, but watch where you put your tent if the forecast calls for rain. Arizona soil does not absorb water easily, and even a little bit of rain can lead to a lot of runoff. Look for telltale drainage trails through the most tempting tent spot.

Outside the loop road near site 6, an overflow area offers extra space, in case you make it all the way to Klondyke and find the campground full. The only time this is likely to happen is during hunting season, when hunters flock here to try for mule deer and javelina.

Klondyke is the eastern gateway to Aravaipa Canyon, 42,000 acres of Nature Conservancy Preserve and BLM-designated wilderness, widely regarded among canyoneers as the best waterside hike in Arizona. Wet-footed hikers enjoy the rare treat of trekking up a spring-fed perennial creek and through an unspoiled natural riparian habitat at the bottom of a deep, scenic canyon. You can hike the 11-mile canyon from one end to the other, or spend a day exploring the side canyons. The BLM issues 50 permits daily—only 20 from the east entrance. Trips are limited to three days (two nights) in the canyon, and reservations can be made three months in advance. Spring and fall are the best times to hike for flora, fauna, and temperature. Fall is particularly beautiful, with the red and yellow leaves of sycamore and cottonwoods reflecting in the clear, blue water. Aravaipa Canyon also forms the seventh segment of the Grand Enchantment Trail, a 700-mile hiking trail network stretching from Phoenix to Albuquerque.

The ranger at the Klondyke station can fill you in on current road and canyon conditions. Unless you have a high-clearance vehicle and are able to make the stream crossings, it is recommended that you park at the information kiosk and restroom and hike the additional 1.5 miles through The Nature Conservancy property to the canyon. If you were unable to secure a permit to hike Aravaipa, you can still hike the Turkey Creek Trail and explore a Salado cliff dwelling from AD 1300.

With your base at Fourmile, you're in a great position to explore two more of Arizona's most remote wildlands. To the northeast is the Santa Theresa Wilderness, characterized by deep, secretive canyons; high, bare ridgelines; and strikingly sculpted granite outcrops. Human presence here is limited to a few rarely used stock trails and a handful of intrepid backpackers, increasing your chances of observing a peregrine falcon, bighorn sheep, black bear, or mountain lion. The 76,000-acre Galiuro Wilderness stretches off to the southwest, mountainsides green with oak and ponderosa. Hike up Rattlesnake Canyon to Powers Garden, and visit the cabin and mine where the unfortunate Power family shot it out with a posse from Safford in 1918. Trails comb the Galiuros, but the little-used tracks can be faint; bring good maps, a compass, and plenty of water, and check in with the Coronado National Forest Safford Ranger District for more information.

Fourmile Canyon Campground

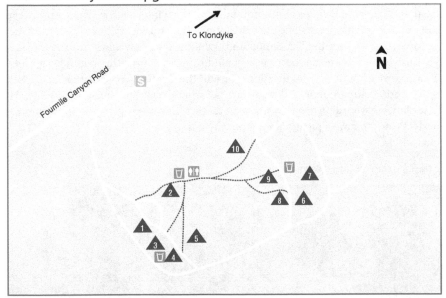

GETTING THERE

From Safford, take US 70 northwest 15 miles to the Aravaipa–Klondyke Road. Turn left and drive southwest 24.5 miles to the junction with the Bonita–Klondyke Road. Turn right and continue northwest 7.5 miles to Klondyke and Fourmile Canyon Road. Turn left and drive southwest 0.5 mile to the campground.

GPS COORDINATES N32° 49.796' W110° 20.744'

44

Hospital Flat Campground

Beauty ★★★★ Privacy ★★★★ Spaciousness ★★★ Quiet ★★★★ Security ★★★ Cleanliness ★★★

Cool temperatures and a beautiful alpine setting are therapeutic.

Driving the 35 miles up the Swift Trail from 2,900 feet elevation to 9,000 feet is ecologically comparable to driving from Mexico to Canada. The road winds its way up the Pinaleño Mountains through saguaros and ocotillos to juniper and pinyons and eventually up to the ferns and towering pines. The Pinaleños (a mixed Apache/Spanish coinage meaning "many deer") are considered a sky island, with the highest peak, Mount Graham, reaching 10,720 feet. The ecosystem at the top of the mountains is so different than the lower desert that the plants and animals here are almost completely isolated from similar populations in other regions. A tremendous variety of wildlife thrive throughout the mountains, and 18 native species have developed here that cannot be found anywhere else.

The Swift Trail, named after the first supervisor of the Coronado National Forest, turns to dirt after 22 miles and closes at this point during the winter season. There are six campgrounds and two picnic areas along the drive, and several opportunities to get out of the car and enjoy the views over the San Simon and Sulphur Springs Valleys. Stop at the Safford Ranger District Office for the route's self-guided tour brochure. The mountain has been a summer retreat since the days of the pioneers, and the Civilian Conservation Corps helped build the roads, campgrounds, and picnic areas. Noon Creek, so named because it was the farthest pioneers were able to get by noon on the first day of a journey up the mountain, is the perfect place to have a picnic and ponder the past.

Hospital Flat is still a healing green haven.

CONTACT: 928-428-4150, tinyurl.com /hospitalflat

OPEN: April 15–November 14, weather and fire conditions permitting

SITES: 11

EACH SITE HAS: Picnic table, fire ring, bearproof box

ASSIGNMENT: First-come, first-served; no reservations

REGISTRATION: Self-register on-site

AMENITIES: Vault toilets, fire rings, nature trail

PARKING: At campsites

FEE: $10/night; $10 day use

ELEVATION: 9,000'

RESTRICTIONS:

PETS: On leash only

FIRES: In fire rings only

ALCOHOL: Permitted

VEHICLES: No RVs or trailers; limit 2 vehicles/site

QUIET HOURS: 10 p.m.–6 a.m.

OTHER: 10-person limit/site; 14-day stay limit; bear-country food-storage restrictions; no drinking water available

Just 1 mile beyond the winter gate is Hospital Flat. In the 1880s this meadow was a field hospital for soldiers from Fort Grant, in the western foothills of Mount Graham. The cool temperatures and beautiful alpine setting were therapeutic for soldiers recovering from hard service in the Apache Wars. The hospital also served as a summer haven for officers and their families. The army operated a signal station from nearby Heliograph Peak. Fort Grant remained in service through the Spanish-American War, then was ceded to Arizona upon statehood and became the State Industrial School for Wayward Boys and Girls; it remains a prison today.

Hospital Flat is the only campground along the Swift Trail designated tent only. All but two sites are set back at least 50 yards from the parking area, requiring a short hike in to your camp. The sites are in the treeline at the edge of a grassy dell filled with bluebells, harebells, and sneezeweed (a lovely little sunflower). A small creek that runs through the meadow must be traversed to get to most of the sites. Sites 10 and 11 combine to form an open and spacious group site, close enough to the parking area that you don't have to worry about hauling your gear or making a midnight hike to the restroom. Sites 8 and 9 are farthest away, downstream where the meadow ends and a small footbridge helps with the sometimes-soggy stream crossing. Site 8 is on the meadow side, with a view and small tent area. A slight rise separates it from site 9, which faces the woods. In either site you fall asleep to the sound of the water gurgling through a small cascade.

Site 7 is a lovely site farther up the meadow from the parking area. It's underneath the trees but doesn't require a creek crossing. One of several faint paths across the meadow leads through site 7 and across the creek to sites 5 and 6. Site 6 is very overgrown and has no picnic table, but site 5 is well screened and shaded with a good, medium-sized tent spot. Our favorite site is 4, which has its own footpath with a small jump over the creek. It's open to great views of the wildflowers in the meadow and provides two sizable tent areas that are shady in the morning. Sites 1, 2, and 3 are closer to the road but site 2 has a nice, shady tent spot with no stream crossing.

A surprise awaits at the end of the Swift Trail, where 11-acre Riggs Flat Lake is stocked with trout for summer fishing. Trails throughout the mountains allow for hiking, biking, and horseback riding, including loops specifically developed for mountain bikers. Particularly notable is the Arcadia Trail 328, which begins at nearby Shannon Campground (another forest gem, and a good alternative if Hospital Flat doesn't suit you).

Atop the highest peak, the Mount Graham International Observatory scans the heavens with some of the world's most sophisticated telescopes. Controversy stirred when the University of Arizona first proposed the observatory, from environmentalists concerned about the habitat of the rare Mount Graham red squirrel, and from Apaches who consider the mountain to have spiritual significance. To find out more and look into the possibility of a tour, stop at Discovery Park on the campus of Eastern Arizona College in Safford.

Hospital Flat Campground

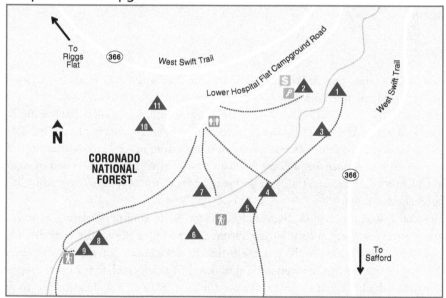

GETTING THERE

From Safford, take US 191 south 8 miles to AZ 366. Turn right and drive southwest 23 miles up the mountain and turn left into the campground.

GPS COORDINATES N32° 40.052' W109° 52.403'

45

Lakeview Campground

Beauty ★★★★ Privacy ★★★ Spaciousness ★★★ Quiet ★★★ Security ★★★ Cleanliness ★★★

Rainbow trout, bass, catfish, and sunfish all wait to be lured out of the depths.

Just 7 miles north of the Mexican border, at the base of the Canelo Hills, sits Parker Canyon Lake. Created by damming the runoff from the Huachuca Mountains, the 132-acre lake now provides bird-watching, boating, and fishing opportunities to anyone wishing to get away from the crowds.

Lakeview Campground, which lives up to its name, has two sections—one for tents and one for RVs. The area specifically for tent campers is on the left as you come in, close to the shore on a grassy hillside. There you'll find 40 sites spread along two loops, each with a picnic table and a fire pit with grill (some have an upright grill). Head into the right-hand loop, but bypass the first 10 sites since you can't see the lake as well from there. Sites 14, 18, 19, and 20 are set down the slope toward the water's edge at the end of the loop. If the grass is tall, you may have trouble spotting the tables that are farther away from the road (it took us several minutes to find site 29).

On the other, smaller loop, four sites are arranged above the parking area and six sites a few steps below. You can easily reach the water from any of the sites by hiking down the hillside. This loop has the feel of a converted picnic area. The tables are a little too close

The wide skies of southern Arizona invite you to take a deep breath and relax.

KEY INFORMATION

CONTACT: 520-378-0311, tinyurl.com
/lakeviewcampground

OPEN: Year-round

SITES: 65

EACH SITE HAS: Picnic table, fire ring

ASSIGNMENT: First-come, first-served;
no reservations

REGISTRATION: Self-register on-site

AMENITIES: Vault toilets, water spigots,
boat ramp, fishing dock, group site,
camp host, general store, boat rentals,
wheelchair-accessible sites

PARKING: At campsites

FEE: $10/night; $10 day use

ELEVATION: 5,400'

RESTRICTIONS:

PETS: On leash only

FIRES: In fire rings only

ALCOHOL: Permitted

VEHICLES: No RVs or trailers in tent loop;
36-foot length limit; 2 vehicles/site; motorbikes restricted to entering/exiting campsite

QUIET HOURS: 10 p.m.–6 a.m.

OTHER: 14-day stay limit; 8-horsepower
boat-motor limit; bear-country food-
storage restrictions; no horses

together, and the sites lack clearly defined tent pads, but even so our favorite site is here—number 32. Spacious, with room for a large tent, it is the farthest down and has a 180° view of the lake below. The landscape here is typical of the Upper Sonoran life zone, and the grasslands are dotted with mature junipers and oaks that provide some shade. The summer houses and cabins on the far side of the lake seem strange, since so many of Arizona's lakes are entirely on federal land, but it helps you imagine you've been invited to a private ranch.

If you're more interested in privacy than a view, and if the campground's not very full, take a look at the sites across the road. This is nominally the RV section, but some of the sites have nice tent areas and there's a bit more brush for screening and shade. Camping outside of the designated sites is prohibited at Parker Canyon Lake.

Just down the road is the boat ramp and fishing dock. The general store offers a chance to purchase forgotten items, but it is closed on Wednesdays during the summer and from Tuesday through Thursday in the winter. Several boats are available for rent. Parker Canyon Lake makes a good year-round destination, and during hunting season, expect to see the sites filled with folks in various states of camouflage. The lake is always popular with anglers; rainbow trout, bass, catfish, and sunfish all wait to be lured out of the depths.

The 5-mile Lakeshore Trail 128 travels completely around the lake past cottonwoods, manzanita, and rolling grassy hills. The hike is primarily on level ground, close to the shoreline. Be sure to bring your binoculars and field guide, since you are bound to see a variety of waterfowl and possibly an osprey or an eagle.

The north trailhead of the Arizona Trail's Passage 1 begins at Parker Canyon Lake. From here you can hike 22 miles through the Miller Peak Wilderness to Montezuma Pass, the point along Forest Road 61 where you can reach the other side of the Huachuca Mountains. Passage 2 of the Arizona Trail heads north into the Canelo Hills, connecting with Passage 3 and ending up in Patagonia. Illegal immigration is common in this area, and it is recommended that hikers be aware of their surroundings. Do not camp close to the trail and do not hike alone. Forestry officials also suggest you avoid hiking in the summer since water is scarce and temperatures can be dangerously high. Be prepared for lake-clearing thunderstorms during the summer monsoon months of July–September.

The scenic drive along FR 61 brings you along the southern edge of the Huachuca Mountains with grassy valleys and side canyons below you. From Montezuma Pass, you have a grand overlook of the San Pedro River and San Rafael Valleys and—somewhere down there—the international border. You can see more of Mexico than Arizona from here. In 18 miles, the drive takes you all the way to the Coronado National Memorial, which commemorates 16th-century Spanish explorer Francisco Vásquez de Coronado's expedition from Mexico into the United States. While hiking through the Coronado National Memorial, it's easy to imagine what it must have been like for Coronado to travel this rugged countryside.

On your way to or from Parker Canyon Lake, be sure to stop at the wineries in Sonoita and Elgin. Here you can taste samples of wine made with grapes grown right here in southern Arizona, and if you happen to be there during the Harvest Festival, you can try stomping some grapes yourself.

Lakeview Campground

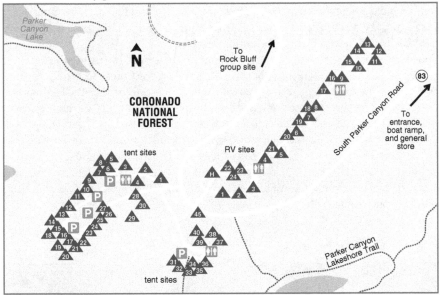

GETTING THERE

From Sierra Vista, take AZ 92 south 14 miles to the Coronado Memorial Road (FR 61). Turn right and head south and west 16 miles to AZ 83. Veer right and drive northwest 5.5 miles to Parker Canyon Lake (AZ 83 becomes South Parker Canyon Road).

From Tucson, take I-10 to AZ 83. Turn right and then continue south 63 miles to Parker Canyon Lake.

GPS COORDINATES N31° 25.690' W110° 27.045'

46

Reef Townsite Campground

Beauty ★★★★ Privacy ★★★ Spaciousness ★★★★ Quiet ★★★ Security ★★★ Cleanliness ★★★★

Miners' cabins once stood where some of these campsites are located today.

From Sierra Vista, you can see the Huachuca Mountains rising like ramparts behind the fort that shares their name. Enter the mountains on Carr Canyon Road, and shortly you find the Carr House Information Center. This former ranch at the base of the hills, which is open on weekends, offers exhibits on area flora, fauna, and history. You can hike the nature trail at any time. After the information center the road continues, switchbacking up more than 2,000 feet past occasional waterfalls and splendid views over the San Pedro River valley. On your way up, look for the Carr Reef, a band of sheer, white quartzite running along the mountainside. Prospectors looked at this formation and saw dollar signs, since quartzite is often an indicator of gold beneath; in fact, miners harvested gold, silver, tungsten, and quartz from these mountains. The reef gave its name to the mining town that sprang up here, which in turn passed it on to the campground.

Ponderosa pine, alligator juniper, and Douglas-fir shade Reef Townsite, while manzanita and silverleaf oak provide screening between the well-spaced sites; according to the U.S. Forest Service, some sites are exactly where miners' cabins once stood. The campground is a pair of loops, numbered counterclockwise, with sites 16, 15, 1, and 2 at the higher end of the sloping townsite. Sites 3, 5, 7, 8, and 9 back up to a small wash, which offers a pleasant soundtrack when water is flowing. Surrounded by manzanita, site 14 sits by itself, overlooking sites 10 and 11. The last small loop, and especially site 13, is quite close to the reservable group site. Our favorite is site 12, from which you can climb a short trail to a picnic table at your very own private overlook. Whichever site you choose, a cleared and leveled tent pad makes for a comfortable night.

Reef's miners once enjoyed this view on their way to a hard day's work.

KEY INFORMATION

CONTACT: 520-378-0311, tinyurl.com
/reeftownsite; reservations: 877-444-6777,
recreation.gov

OPEN: April–November

SITES: 16

EACH SITE HAS: Picnic table, fire ring;
some have an upright grill, bearproof box

ASSIGNMENT: First-come, first-served;
reservations accepted for group site

REGISTRATION: Self-register on-site

AMENITIES: Vault toilets, water spigots

PARKING: At campsites

FEE: $10/night standard sites, $45/night
group site; $10 day use

ELEVATION: 7,200'

RESTRICTIONS:

PETS: On leash only

FIRES: In fire rings only

ALCOHOL: Permitted

VEHICLES: 12-foot trailer limit; 20-foot
vehicle limit; 2 vehicles/site; motorized
and mechanized vehicles, including
mountain bikes, prohibited in wilderness

QUIET HOURS: 10 p.m.–6 a.m.

OTHER: 14-day stay limit; bear-country
food-storage restrictions; firearms
prohibited; horses prohibited; 10-person
limit/site

To learn more about the history of Reef, hike the 0.7-mile Reef Historic Trail, which begins and ends near site 12. As interpretive signs describe geologic features and the activities of the Exposed Reef Mining Company, spectacular views of Carr Canyon unfold below. The trail was originally a mining road, and you can compare the landscape you see now with photographs of Reef's mining heyday.

If Reef Townsite Campground is full, or simply not high enough for you, continue to Ramsey Vista Campground. Most of the 8 sites are closer together and more exposed to one another than at Reef Townsite, but sites 1, 2, and 4 on the outside of the loop have an open mountaintop feeling and views of the surrounding heights. A corral is located near site 1, but horses are not recommended on many of the trails, including Carr Peak Trail. Horses are not permitted in Reef Townsite.

Two trailheads (one across the road from the Reef Townsite Campground entrance, the other just before you get to Ramsey Vista Campground) give you access to the network of trails leading through the Miller Peak Wilderness and up to Carr Peak (9,230') or Miller Peak (9,466'). Trails include the Comfort Springs Trail 109, which leaves Ramsey Vista and heads downhill through Carr Canyon and Ramsey Canyon and, if connected with Hamburg Trail 122, all the way to Ramsey Canyon Preserve. Make arrangements to leave a vehicle at the preserve and you can hike all the way down, spend the day at this lush riparian oasis, and drive back up to your campsite.

Because of the canyon's direction, its walls' height, and the occurrence of a spring-fed stream, Ramsey Canyon is wet and cool, making a perfect habitat for a wide variety of plant and animal life. More than 170 bird species are found in the preserve, and the hummingbird observation area is one of the best places to see 17 different species of hummers. Stop by in the morning and catch a guided nature walk; you may catch a glimpse of a coatimundi, a relative of the raccoon found only in the Southwest. The Nature Conservancy manages the preserve and collects a $6 fee per person; it's closed on holidays and on Tuesdays and Wednesdays during the winter.

Save some time in your itinerary to visit Fort Huachuca, which has an unbroken history of military service from 1877 to today. The Fort Huachuca Museum includes exhibits about the Buffalo Soldiers, the campaign against Geronimo, and daily life in the frontier army, while the US Army Intelligence Museum covers more modern aspects of the military mission.

Nearby, San Pedro Riparian National Conservation Area—57,000 acres of land along the San Pedro River—is home to 350 species of birds and more than 80 species of mammals. Check the hike schedule to join guided treks to see Arizona's largest cottonwood, the Hohokam petroglyphs, or the ruins of abandoned mills.

Historic Tombstone, the infamous "Town Too Tough to Die," is also just up the way. There you can relive the gunfight at the O.K. Corral, join a ghost tour of the historic buildings (including the notorious Bird Cage Theatre, now a museum), or have a drink at one of the many saloons.

Reef Townsite Campground

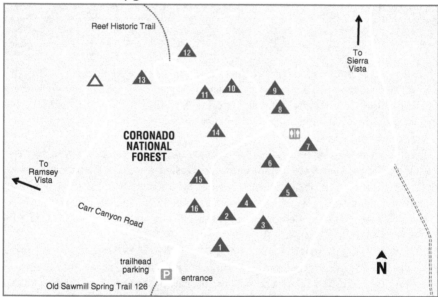

GETTING THERE

From Sierra Vista, take AZ 92 south to Carr Canyon Road. Turn right and continue up the mountain 6.5 miles to the campground entrance.

GPS COORDINATES N31° 25.689' W110° 17.441'

47

Riverview Campground

Beauty ★★★ Privacy ★★★★ Spaciousness ★★★★ Quiet ★★★★★ Security ★★★★ Cleanliness ★★★★

Gila River and Bonita Creek form a 35-mile corridor of rare and precious habitat filled with plant and animal life.

The Gila Box National Riparian Conservation Area (NRCA) was designated in 1990, one of only two such areas in the nation. Gila River and Bonita Creek form a 35-mile corridor of rare and precious habitat filled with plant and animal life. Along the water, massive cottonwoods, broad-leaved sycamores, and willow and walnut trees shade lush banks, rocky riffles, and sandy beaches. In the Box, sheer cliffs rise above the river, exposed rock layers telling the tale of eons of intermittent volcanic upheaval.

Two campgrounds bookend the Gila Box—Owl Creek on the eastern end and Riverview on the west—about 23 river-miles apart. Both are located on desert terrain just outside the fragile riparian corridor, with views of the Gila winding below. If you're a paddler, leave your shuttle car at Dry Canyon Boat Take Out and spend the night at Owl Creek. Head downstream in the morning to get the best of what the Box has to offer. If the river's flowing fast, you can make it a day trip, or dawdle a bit and spend a night along the way. Primitive camping is allowed throughout the NRCA, with restrictions in the riparian zone. Visit the

Ocotillo and other desert plants surround the campground while verdant riparian foliage lines the river.

KEY INFORMATION

CONTACT: 928-348-4400, blm.gov/visit/riverview-campground

OPEN: Year-round

SITES: 13

EACH SITE HAS: Picnic table, fire ring, upright grill, ramada

ASSIGNMENT: First-come, first-served; no reservations

REGISTRATION: Self-register on-site

AMENITIES: Vault toilets, water spigots

PARKING: At campsites

FEE: $5/night, $3/person to float, $2/additional vehicle

ELEVATION: 3,300'

RESTRICTIONS:

PETS: On leash only

FIRES: In fire rings only

ALCOHOL: Permitted

VEHICLES: No length limit; 2 vehicles/site

QUIET HOURS: 10 p.m.–6 a.m.

OTHER: 14-day stay limit; downed and dead firewood collection only; discharging of firearms prohibited; checkout time 11 a.m.; glass containers prohibited in or along shorelines or creeks

U.S. Geological Survey website at waterdata.usgs.gov/az/nwis/current/?type=flow to check current water flow and contact the Bureau of Land Management for information and regulations. Water flow levels will determine the speed, difficulty, and degree of excitement of your trip.

If you can't do the full float or you've got other activities in mind, make your base at the Riverview Campground. The desert is a little greener here than at Owl Creek, the sites are farther apart, and river access is easier. The road in is partially paved, and while it's quite curvy, it's perfectly passable. This is one of the newer campgrounds we've seen, and while it may have less charm than an old Civilian Conservation Corps site, it's also seen 80 fewer years of wear and tear. The fire rings are clearly new with attached grills that move easily, and the sturdy concrete picnic tables show no abuse. Riverview sites also come complete with upright grills for barbecuing and a small shade ramada at each site to tame the midday sun.

The first seven sites are all very similar, lined up about 200 feet apart and at least that far from the road, overlooking the canyon. Opposite, the sheer cliffs rise 500 feet from the river, reflecting the sound of rushing water. Each site follows the same pattern, with ramada and picnic table in the center, fire ring on the left and grill on the right. Between the sites, prickly pear, ocotillo, mesquite, paloverde, creosote, barrel cactus, and cholla thrive. Due to the rocky ground and the profusion of spiny plants, you'll be most comfortable tenting (with a good mattress under you) in the generous gravel area.

Sites 8–13 follow the looping road that mimics the bend in the canyon, and all except 12 and 13 have a view of the river to the west. Site 8 is a wide site on the corner where the road branches off to the river-access and day-use areas and could easily accommodate a large group. Tall ocotillos surround site 10, the tips of their branches ready to burst into flame with spring blossoms. The last three sites have pull-throughs, and site 11 best suits pop-ups or truck campers since it's the only one without a tent spot of any kind. One set of toilets serves the campground, and it's quite a hike from sites 7, 8, and 9. If you're concerned about making the trek in the middle of the night, consider sites 2, 3, or 13.

At this elevation, desert camping means hot, hot summers and cold winter nights. Come in March for the wildflower bloom, or in fall to hike the canyon bottom under cottonwoods and sycamores blazing with color; in either season you'll find a plethora of migrating birds taking advantage of the oasis. Golden eagles soar year-round, and canyon natives include beaver, javelina, and bighorn sheep. If you're lucky, you may glimpse a mountain lion.

The best hiking is along the watercourses, although high water in the Gila may restrict how far you can safely go. From Riverview, you've got a good base to explore Bonita Creek, where native fish still predominate in the perennial stream. For nonhikers, the Bonita Creek Watchable Wildlife area provides an accessible place to sit and overlook the canyon and is a great perch to look for birds in the leafy canopy. The Serna Cabin picnic area nearby will help you imagine river-bottom life. Hohokam, Mogollon, Anasazi, and Apache all hunted and farmed in these narrow canyons over the last millennium, and the Box was a well-known route for travelers. Early in the 20th century, more than 40 small family farms dotted what is now the NRCA, the Serna homestead among them.

If you've brought your kayak but aren't up for a long trip, you can put in at Serna Cabin picnic area and paddle down to the Dry Canyon Boat Take Out. If land-based recreation is more your thing, you'll find miles and miles of scenic back roads in and around the Gila Box, ranging from well maintained to quite primitive.

Riverview Campground

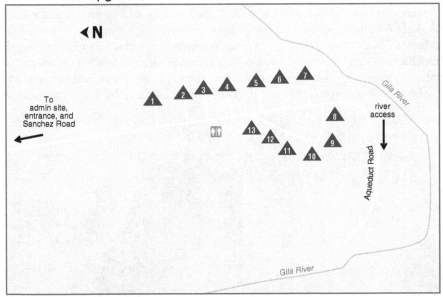

GETTING THERE

From Safford, take US 70 east for 5 miles to Sanchez Road. Turn left and head northeast 12 miles, following the signs to the campground.

GPS COORDINATES N32° 53.320' W109° 28.798'

48

⛺ Spencer Canyon Campground

Beauty ★★★ Privacy ★★★ Spaciousness ★★★ Quiet ★★★ Security ★★★★ Cleanliness ★★★★

The four camping areas here each have their own personality.

The Santa Catalina Mountains are one of Arizona's sky islands—isolated mountains rising thousands of feet above the surrounding sea of desert. They are moist, green havens for plants and animals unable to tolerate the searing heat below and now left stranded by millennia of climate change. Biologists say the 28-mile drive from Tucson to the top of Mount Lemmon is, ecologically, like a trip from Mexico to Canada. Awaking to fog and mist at Spencer Canyon Campground, we certainly felt like we could be in Washington State, until we realized we were just inside a cloud.

The Catalina Highway is a designated scenic drive—the Sky Island Parkway—and is a Tucsonian's only access to this cool respite from summer's heat. As you start to climb, the Tucson valley sprawls out below you, and canyons ripple off into the distance like sand shaped by the ocean waves. Pull over and enjoy the view from the Babad Do'ag Vista, which is a great spot to watch the sunset and see the city lights brighten the night.

You can make several neat stops along the drive, including the interpretive trail at Gordon Hirabayashi Campground, once a minimum-security federal honor camp. Hirabayashi, a Japanese American who objected to wartime internment, epitomized an honor prisoner—he hitchhiked to Arizona on his own recognizance when authorities failed to provide transportation (or even train fare) after his trial. The Catalina Highway was built primarily by the men who served their sentences here. If there's been rain lately, the Seven Cataracts Vista

A mile and a half of elevation makes for cool weather and spectacular views.

KEY INFORMATION

CONTACT: 520-749-8700, tinyurl.com/spencercanyon

OPEN: April–October 15

SITES: 66

EACH SITE HAS: Picnic table, fire ring, some have an upright grill, bearproof box

ASSIGNMENT: First-come, first-served; no reservations

REGISTRATION: Self-register on-site

AMENITIES: Vault toilets, water spigots, campground host, firewood, wheelchair-accessible sites

PARKING: At campsites

FEE: $22/night single, $36/night double, $9/additional vehicle; $10 day use

ELEVATION: 8,000'

RESTRICTIONS:

PETS: On leash only; prohibited in the Pusch Ridge Wilderness

FIRES: In fire rings only

ALCOHOL: Permitted

VEHICLES: 22-foot length limit; ATVs prohibited, motorized vehicles and bicycles prohibited in Pusch Ridge Wilderness

QUIET HOURS: 10 p.m.–6 a.m.

OTHER: 14-day stay limit; bear-country food-storage restrictions; firearms prohibited; horses prohibited

lets you peek at the seven waterfalls of Sabino Canyon. A 7.8-mile hike originating in the Sabino Canyon Recreation Area will take you to the base of the cataracts—after multiple wet stream crossings.

Farther up, unpack your tackle for Rose Canyon Lake, a seven-acre no-boating lake stocked with rainbow trout, and one of the most popular places on the mountain. The 76 somewhat-crowded campsites here are heavily used and fill up early. Keep on to Spencer Canyon Campground, the highest of the area's five campgrounds at 8,000 feet, where the host brags that once regulars spend a night here, they won't pitch their tents anywhere else.

Enjoy your trip up the mountain, but don't tarry too long. Many of the campsites at Spencer Canyon are far enough off the road that they'd be difficult to find after dark. There are four camping areas—Ponderosa Loop, East Fork, Spencer Loop, and Turkey Track. It's almost as if there are four different campgrounds, each with its own personality. Ponderosa Loop is the first and smallest with seven sites, two of which belong to the resident camp host. Sites 6 and 7 are well apart, downhill from the road among the tall pines. At East Fork, nine walk-in sites dot a rocky patch of forest. Site 16 is cute and private, with a fine hearth built into the boulders.

Spencer Loop, the largest of the four areas, offers several good sites on the slopes among the ponderosas. You may have to hunt for the leveled tent spot in the steeper sites—it's often uphill. Many of the sites throughout Spencer Canyon have steep, tricky access, so keep your flashlight handy.

Turkey Track is farthest in, with several great sites and our favorite spot—site 57. This large, private site is at the end of the loop, hidden past sites 56 and 58. A short hike from here takes you to your own rocky overlook, where you can see the city lights of Tucson miles below.

Between Rose and Spencer canyons, you pass the U.S. Forest Service Palisade Visitor Center, the place to find information on all the terrific hikes in the 56,933-acre Pusch Ridge Wilderness, as well as to brush up on local wildlife. Deer are everywhere, along with fancy Abert's squirrels and nosy Steller's jays, and black bears and mountain lions also prowl here.

At the top of the mountain lies the town of Summerhaven, which has made an amazing recovery from the devastating Aspen Fire of 2003. Stop by the Mt. Lemmon General Store for some homemade fudge and souvenirs, or dine at the Cookie Cabin and Pizzeria. After a chilly evening in camp, you can also have a warm breakfast at the Iron Door Restaurant in Ski Valley and take a scenic ski lift ride.

Be prepared for heavy rains during July–September, and bring your long johns in spring and fall. It's hard to imagine freezing when it's 80°F in the desert, but on one March trip we saw people shoveling snow into the beds of their pickups to haul it back to Tucson.

For an adventurous trip home, take the Control Road (Forest Road 38) to Oracle down the north side of the mountains. When I asked at the Mt. Lemmon General Store if the Oracle Road was open, the grinning clerk replied, "Sure . . . if you have a rental car." The road can be steep, narrow, and rough, and four-wheel drive is required, but it is a lovely drive.

Spencer Canyon Campground

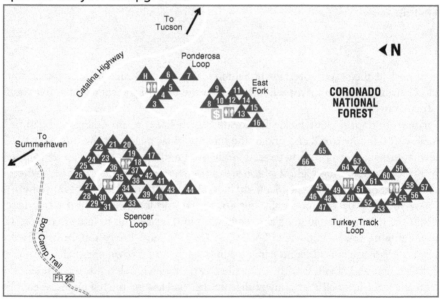

GETTING THERE

From Tucson, go east on Tanque Verde to Catalina Highway. Turn left and travel north 4.2 miles to the national forest boundary. Continue up Mount Lemmon 21 miles to the campground entrance. Turn left into the campground.

GPS COORDINATES N32° 25.117' W110° 44.300'

49

Stockton Pass Campground

Beauty ★★★ Privacy ★★★★ Spaciousness ★★★★ Quiet ★★★★ Security ★★ Cleanliness ★★★

This secluded campground is in a lovely open woodland at the base of the Pinaleño Mountains.

Eastern Arizona is the land of the Three C's: copper, cotton, and cattle, all of which are well represented in the Safford area. Stockton Pass was once the eastern gateway to Aravaipa Canyon and the Sulphur Springs Valley, where the third *C* reigned supreme. Marshall Trimble, in *Roadside History of Arizona,* called this the "richest cattle country in the West," miles and miles of prime grazing land fed by the rains and snows of the Pinaleño, Galiuro, and Chiricahua Mountains. AZ 266 loops around the southern end of the Pinaleños, slipping through Stockton Pass on its way to Bonita, once a thriving town of 1,000 souls. Its 10 saloons and several bawdy houses were frequented by prospectors, cowboys, and soldiers from nearby Fort Grant. Today Bonita is a ghost town, Fort Grant is a state prison, and the tall grass that brushed the stirrups of pioneers grows shorter and sparser among prickly pear, sotol, and cholla.

Old Man Stockton, the pass's namesake, ranched in this area in the 1870s. The U.S. Forest Service identifies Stockton as father of the Clanton brothers, whose feud with the Earps became American legend when bullets flew at the O.K. Corral. We couldn't find the connection ourselves, but Newman Haynes "Old Man" Clanton, a cattle king (and rumored outlaw boss) who ruled the range from the San Pedro River to the Animas Valley in New

Morning highlights Stockton Pass's charms.

KEY INFORMATION

CONTACT: 928-428-4150, tinyurl.com
/stocktonpass

OPEN: Year-round

SITES: 11

EACH SITE HAS: Picnic table, fire ring;
some have an upright grill

ASSIGNMENT: First-come, first-served;
no reservations

REGISTRATION: Not required

AMENITIES: Vault toilets

PARKING: At campsites, in parking lot

FEE: None

ELEVATION: 5,600'

RESTRICTIONS:

PETS: On leash only

FIRES: In fire rings only

ALCOHOL: Permitted

VEHICLES: 22-foot length limit

QUIET HOURS: Not specified

OTHER: 14-day stay limit; bear-country
food-storage restrictions; no drinking
water available

Mexico, must certainly have had a stake in this rich area. From the pass, you can look out over the valleys below and imagine the lives of these frontiersmen.

The discreet sign marking the turnoff to the recreation site shows only a picnic table, and casual passersby might not guess that there is a campground tucked back in here. It's this seclusion that appeals to us, as well as the lovely open woodland at the transition between plains and mountain. Wind in on a rutted, ungraded road past two cattle guards. Eleven sites in seven groups are scattered around the circular parking area, leveled, and defined with stonework in characteristic Civilian Conservation Corps fashion. Mature oak trees and alligator junipers provide shade, and manzanita sprawls between the scattered sites.

Look for site numbers on most of the picnic tables. The first group of tables we take to be site 1/2/3. This large, sunny area has two fire pits, a large bonfire ring, and plenty of room for lots of tents. It's perfect for families, and even comes with an adorable kid-sized stone picnic table. Going around the loop counterclockwise, you'll find site 4 convenient to the parking area and the restroom. Set back up a slight rise is 5/6, a double site with two end-to-end picnic tables and two side-by-side fire pits. Nearby trees provide some early-morning or late-afternoon relief, but these are sunny sites at midday.

For deeper shade, choose 7/8, another double site that sits two steps down in a sunken-living-room arrangement. Make sure you've got a good ground cloth if there's rain threatening—things could get a little soggy here. A large alligator juniper shades site 9. Follow the path leading under the canopy of trees behind site 9 and you'll find enchanting and secretive site 10. There's afternoon shade, a large, bermed tent spot, and an added upright grill. The last site, 11, backs up against a hillside just off its own parking tab. The site itself is compact, level, and nicely laid out, although the tent spots are small and uneven.

Above the grassy slopes to the north loom the pine-capped Pinaleños. The Shake Trail climbs steadily from the campground, up 3,000 feet in less than 5 miles, meeting the Swift Trail near the ridgeline. The effort takes you to beautiful mountain meadows and into deep evergreen forest. Hike up or down with a car shuttle, but you'll need a good guide to help you find the unmarked upper trailhead. Stockton Pass makes a good base to explore the mountains, with far less traffic than the busy campgrounds along the Swift Trail (for more about the Pinaleños, see profile 42, Hospital Flat Campground, page 148).

The edge is off the summer heat here at 5,600 feet, although you'll still appreciate what shade you can find. Spring is really the season to visit, when the hills are carpeted with wildflowers. Fall can also be very pleasant, even when snow has already brushed the peaks; winter campers should come prepared for cold nights. There are black bears aplenty in the Pinaleños, so keep a clean camp and don't attract a wanderer. Mule deer also pick their delicate way through the campground, and skunks and squirrels abound. It's quiet here, so enjoy nature's night sounds, but don't be alarmed: the weird, plaintive bawling drowning out the coyotes is only lowing cattle. Remember your telescope, too, because once the sun goes down, you'll see why the Pinaleño Mountains host the Mount Graham International Observatory. If you start to feel too lonesome in this remote area, you can backtrack to US 191 and stop at Roper Lake State Park, which offers fine fishing, rental cabins, and a natural hot spring tub.

Stockton Pass Campground

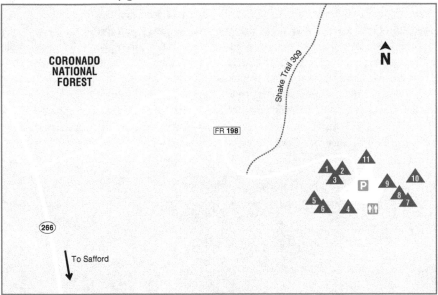

GETTING THERE

From Safford, take US 191 south 17 miles to AZ 266. Turn right and drive west 12 miles to campground entrance. Turn right into the campground.

GPS COORDINATES N32° 35.511' W109° 51.291'

Sunny Flat Campground

Beauty ★★★★ Privacy ★★★ Spaciousness ★★★ Quiet ★★★ Security ★★★ Cleanliness ★★★★

The Chiricahua Mountains are a wonderland of weathered crevices, precarious balancing rocks, and eerie hoodoos.

There's a deep mystery in southern Arizona, and if you cross the state on I-10, you'll see the signs—literally. Vivid yellow billboards asking only THE THING. WHAT IS IT? adorn the roadside from Tucson to New Mexico, alternating with the barrel's end view of a gunfighter, cordially inviting you to Tombstone.

You'll find plenty of mystery in these parts, but some of the most impressive history doesn't involve six-guns and shoot-outs. Head for the Chiricahua Mountains from the west and you can't miss Texas Canyon, whose boulders give you a taste of the geologic dramas that have taken place here. Look to the south for the distinctive two-headed peak of Dos Cabeza Mountains. Farther east, the Chiricahua Mountains tower in the distance, their tallest peak at 9,797 feet. There 87,700 acres of wilderness top the rugged volcanic sky island, including a wonderland of weathered crevices, precarious balancing rocks, and eerie hoodoos that form Chiricahua National Monument.

Swing around the mountains to the east side, to the tiny town of Portal, and enter the wilderness through Cave Creek Canyon. Make a quick stop at the visitor center to pick up trail information, and make sure to get a bird list. More than 300 bird species make their home in the Chiricahuas, and Cave Creek is famous for its bird-watching.

Interesting geology abounds on both sides of the Chiricahua range.

KEY INFORMATION

CONTACT: 520-388-8436, tinyurl.com /sunnyflat

OPEN: April–October

SITES: 12

EACH SITE HAS: Picnic table, fire ring, bearproof box, lantern hook

ASSIGNMENT: First-come, first-served; no reservations

REGISTRATION: Self-register on-site

AMENITIES: Vault toilets, water spigots, camp host

PARKING: At campsites

FEE: $10/night; $10 day use; $5 trailhead parking

ELEVATION: 5,200'

RESTRICTIONS:

PETS: On leash only

FIRES: In fire rings only

ALCOHOL: Permitted

VEHICLES: 28-foot length limit; 16-foot length limit on road; 2 vehicles/site

QUIET HOURS: 10 p.m.–6 a.m.

OTHER: 14-day stay limit; pack in/pack out; bear-country food-storage restrictions; discharging of firearms prohibited; horses prohibited; 10-person limit/site

The first campground you come to is Idlewilde, across a concrete bridge over the perennial creek. This lovely campground set between a sycamore-lined creek and lichen-covered boulders is a perfect choice if it is open. Recent flooding events have prompted closures during the summer monsoon season, so be sure to check with the U.S. Forest Service before heading out.

The second campground in the Cave Creek Recreation Area is Stewart. It provides 6 shaded sites in a small loop ideal for tent campers, but we recommend you travel a bit farther to Sunny Flat, the most popular of the Cave Creek campgrounds. At Sunny Flat you'll find 12 sites near the perennial creek shaded by sheer, peach-colored cliffs. Sites 1–6 flank the road and, although close to one another, offer good tent spots and plenty of shade. We prefer the sites on the outside of the camp loop. Site 9, our favorite, is particularly spacious and private, and has an easy ramble to the creek. Trails run from the campground to the information center and to a nearby vista point.

If you come during the busiest season, March–April, and find the campground full, dispersed camping is also available at John Hands and Herb Martyr. These former camp-grounds have been converted to day-use or dispersed areas after they were damaged by major flooding during 2014's hurricane Odile. Additional dispersed camping is available once you get outside of the recreation area. One sign you'll see throughout southern Arizona reads SMUGGLING AND ILLEGAL IMMIGRATION MAY BE ENCOUNTERED IN THIS AREA. While problems are rare for campers and hikers, especially in developed areas, authorities recommend not hiking alone and avoiding areas where there are well-used unofficial trails and signs of debris from border crossers.

While in the Chiricahuas, be sure to set aside a day to visit the Chiricahua National Monument. Compacted ash laid down by a volcanic eruption 27 million years ago formed the rocks of this area. Erosion in the intervening eons has created striking stone spires and wild boulder-balancing acts. To get a small taste, drive the 8-mile Bonita Canyon Drive to Massai Point. If you have more time, take a hike and wander through rock formations with names such as Sea Captain, Duck on a Rock, and Punch and Judy. Loop hikes of varying lengths take you through Echo Canyon, Totem Canyon, or into the Heart of Rocks. The drive from the campground takes you along Pinery Canyon Scenic Drive (Forest Road 42). The dirt road is passable by standard passenger cars in dry conditions, although high clearance is still recommended.

Cave Creek also boasts South Fork Zoological and Botanical Area, world famous for its bird-watching and wildlife viewing, and well worth the $5 day-use fee. Listen for the barking call of the elegant trogon. This beautiful bird with a bright red belly, white chest band, and brilliant emerald head only enters the United States along the Mexican border, and this is one of the best places to see it. (Professional bird-watchers take note: use of recorded calls to attract the birds is not allowed here during the breeding months.) The American Museum of Natural History's Southwest Research Station is also located nearby. Scientists work here, but visitors are welcome to bird-watch—seven-day birding tours are available, and volunteers are always needed.

Are you still wondering about The Thing? Well, if you have a taste for the odd, off-beat, kitschy, and slightly hokey, it's well worth the $1 price of admission for this classic American roadside attraction.

Sunny Flat Campground

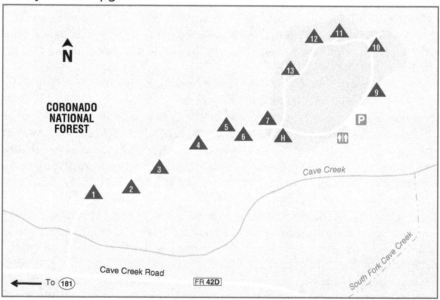

GETTING THERE

From Willcox, take AZ 186 south 31 miles to AZ 181. Turn left and drive 3 miles to FR 42. Turn right and drive 12 miles to the Onion Saddle. Turn right onto FR 42D/Cave Creek Road, and continue 3 miles to the campground.

GPS COORDINATES N31° 53.020' W109° 10.680'

APPENDIX A

CAMPING EQUIPMENT CHECKLIST

Camping is more fun when you can enjoy it at a moment's notice—after all, you never know when the opportunity may arise to head for the woods. And when it does, wouldn't it be nice to be able to pack your car with all the essentials drawn from prepacked boxes carefully cleaned, resupplied, and stored after your last trip?

COOKING/KITCHEN STUFF
Bottle opener
Bottles of salt, pepper, spices, sugar, cooking
    oil, and pancake syrup in waterproof,
    spillproof containers
Bowls
Can opener
Cooking pots with lids
Cooler
Corkscrew
Cups, plastic or tin
Dish soap (biodegradable), dishcloth, and towel
Dutch oven and fire pan
Fire starter
Flatware
Food of your choice
Frying pan and spatula
Fuel for stove
Lighter, matches in waterproof container
Paper towels
Plates
Pocketknife
Stove and fuel
Strainer
Tablecloth
Tinfoil
Trash bags
Wooden spoon

SLEEPING GEAR
Pillow
Sleeping bag
Sleeping pad (inflatable or insulated)
Tent with ground tarp and rainfly

MISCELLANEOUS
Bath soap (biodegradable), washcloth, and towel
Camp chairs
Candles
Day pack
Extra batteries
First aid kit (see page 5)
Flashlight/headlamp
Lantern
Maps (road, trail, topographic, etc.)
Moist towelettes
Saw/ax
Sunglasses
Toilet paper
Water bottle(s)
Wool blanket
Zip-top plastic bags

OPTIONAL
Barbecue grill
Binoculars
Books
Camera
Cards and board games
Field guides on bird, plant, and
    wildlife identification
Fishing rod and tackle
Frisbee
GPS unit

APPENDIX B

SOURCES OF INFORMATION

ARIZONA STATE PARKS
23751 N. 23rd Ave., Ste. 190
Phoenix, AZ 85085
602-542-4174, azstateparks.com

BUREAU OF LAND MANAGEMENT
ARIZONA STATE OFFICE
1 N. Central Ave., Ste. 800
Phoenix, AZ 85004-4427
602-417-9200, blm.gov/arizona

NATIONAL PARK SERVICE
GRAND CANYON NATIONAL PARK
P.O. Box 129
Grand Canyon, AZ 86023
928-638-7888, nps.gov/grca

NAVAJO NATIONAL MONUMENT
PO Box 7717
Shonto, AZ 86045
928-672-2700, nps.gov/nava

ORGAN PIPE CACTUS NATIONAL MONUMENT
10 Organ Pipe Dr.
Ajo, AZ 85321
520-387-6849, nps.gov/orpi

U.S. FOREST SERVICE
APACHE-SITGREAVES NATIONAL FOREST
30 S. Chiricahua Dr.
Springerville, AZ 85938
928-333-6280, fs.usda.gov/asnf

COCONINO NATIONAL FOREST
1824 S. Thompson St.
Flagstaff, AZ 86001
928-527-3600, fs.usda.gov/coconino

CORONADO NATIONAL FOREST
300 W. Congress St.
Tucson, AZ 85701
520-388-8300, fs.usda.gov/coronado

KAIBAB NATIONAL FOREST
800 S. Sixth St.
Williams, AZ 86046
928-635-8200, fs.usda.gov/kaibab

PRESCOTT NATIONAL FOREST
344 S. Cortez St.
Prescott, AZ 86303
928-443-8000, fs.usda.gov/prescott

TONTO NATIONAL FOREST
2324 E. McDowell Rd.
Phoenix, AZ 85006
602-225-5200, fs.usda.gov/tonto

MARICOPA COUNTY PARKS AND RECREATION
41835 N. Castle Hot Springs Rd.
Morristown, AZ 85342
602-506-2930, maricopacountyparks.net

THE NATURE CONSERVANCY IN ARIZONA
7600 N. 15th St., Ste. 100
Phoenix, AZ 85020
602-712-0048, nature.org/arizona

NAVAJO NATION PARKS & RECREATION
PO Box 2520
Window Rock, AZ 86515
928-871-6647, navajonationparks.org

WHITE MOUNTAIN APACHE TRIBE
WILDLIFE AND OUTDOOR RECREATION DIVISION
201 E. Walnut St.
Whiteriver, AZ 85941
928-338-4346, wmatoutdoors.org

INDEX

ABOUT THE AUTHORS

Kirstin Olmon Phillips and Kelly Phillips, both transplants from other parts of the United States, fell in love with Arizona from the first saguaro. Now they combine 37 years of experience roaming the Grand Canyon State's many landscapes. They live in Flagstaff with their dog, Luna, in a house that never gets cleaned on weekends, when trip planning often consists of just hopping in the truck and picking a promising dotted line on the map. They never tire of providing vicarious adventures for friends and are thrilled to share Arizona's wonders with a wider audience.

Photo: Gary Alpert

DEAR CUSTOMERS AND FRIENDS,

SUPPORTING YOUR INTEREST IN OUTDOOR ADVENTURE, travel, and an active lifestyle is central to our operations, from the authors we choose to the locations we detail to the way we design our books. Menasha Ridge Press was incorporated in 1982 by a group of veteran outdoorsmen and professional outfitters. For many years now, we've specialized in creating books that benefit the outdoors enthusiast.

Almost immediately, Menasha Ridge Press earned a reputation for revolutionizing outdoors- and travel-guidebook publishing. For such activities as canoeing, kayaking, hiking, backpacking, and mountain biking, we established new standards of quality that transformed the whole genre, resulting in outdoor-recreation guides of great sophistication and solid content. Menasha Ridge Press continues to be outdoor publishing's greatest innovator.

The folks at Menasha Ridge Press are as at home on a whitewater river or mountain trail as they are editing a manuscript. The books we build for you are the best they can be, because we're responding to your needs. Plus, we use and depend on them ourselves.

We look forward to seeing you on the river or the trail. If you'd like to contact us directly, visit us at menasharidge.com. We thank you for your interest in our books and the natural world around us all.

SAFE TRAVELS,

Bob Sehlinger

**BOB SEHLINGER
PUBLISHER**